Embodied
Inquiry

BLOOMSBURY RESEARCH METHODS

Edited by Graham Crow and Mark Elliot

The Bloomsbury Research Methods series provides authoritative introductions to a range of research methods which are at the forefront of developments in a range of disciplines.

Each volume sets out the key elements of the particular method and features examples of its application, drawing on a consistent structure across the whole series. Written in an accessible style by leading experts in the field, this series is an innovative pedagogical and research resource.

Also available in the series

Community Studies, Graham Crow
Diary Method, Ruth Bartlett and Christine Milligan
GIS, Nick Bearman
Inclusive Research, Melanie Nind
Qualitative Longitudinal Research, Bren Neale
Quantitative Longitudinal Data Analysis, Vernon Gayle and
    Paul Lambert
Rhythmanalysis, Dawn Lyon

Forthcoming in the series

Statistical Modelling in R, Kevin Ralston, Vernon Gayle, Roxanne
    Connelly and Chris Playford

RESEARCH METHODS

Embodied Inquiry

JENNIFER LEIGH AND
NICOLE BROWN

BLOOMSBURY ACADEMIC
LONDON • NEW YORK • OXFORD • NEW DELHI • SYDNEY

BLOOMSBURY ACADEMIC
Bloomsbury Publishing Plc
50 Bedford Square, London, WC1B 3DP, UK
1385 Broadway, New York, NY 10018, USA
29 Earlsfort Terrace, Dublin 2, Ireland

BLOOMSBURY, BLOOMSBURY ACADEMIC and the Diana logo are trademarks
of Bloomsbury Publishing Plc

First published in Great Britain 2021

Series design: Charlotte James
Cover image: © shuoshu / iStock

A catalogue record for this book is available from the British Library.

Library of Congress Cataloging-in-Publication Data.
Names: Leigh, Jennifer, 1976- author. | Brown, Nicole, author.
Title: Embodied inquiry: research methods / Jennifer Leigh and Nicole Brown.
Description: London; New York: Bloomsbury Academic, 2021. | Series:
Bloomsbury research methods | Includes bibliographical references and index. |
Identifiers: LCCN 2020055544 (print) | LCCN 2020055545 (ebook) |
ISBN 9781350118775 (hardback) | ISBN 9781350118768 (paperback) |
ISBN 9781350118782 (epub) | ISBN 9781350118799 (ebook)
Subjects: LCSH: Qualitative research–Methodology. | Social sciences–
Research–Philosophy. | Social sciences–Research–Moral and ethical aspects. |
Awareness. | Self-knowledge, Theory of. | Movement, Psychology of.
Classification: LCC H62 .L4246 2021 (print) | LCC H62 (ebook) |
DDC 001.4/2–dc23
LC record available at https://lccn.loc.gov/2020055544
LC ebook record available at https://lccn.loc.gov/2020055545

ISBN PB: 978-1-3501-1876-8
       HB: 978-1-3501-1877-5
     ePDF: 978-1-3501-1879-9
    eBook: 978-1-3501-1878-2

Series: Bloomsbury Research Methods

Typeset by Deanta Global Publishing Services, Chennai, India

To find out more about our authors and books visit www.bloomsbury.com
and sign up for our newsletters.

CONTENTS

FIGURES

AUTHOR BIOS

Nicole Brown is a lecturer in education and academic head of Learning and Teaching at UCL Institute of Education and Director of Social Research & Practice in Education Ltd.
nicole.brown@ucl.ac.uk
Nicole gained her PhD at the University of Kent for her research into the construction of academic identity under the influence of fibromyalgia. Her editorial work includes *Ableism in Academia: Theorising Disabilities and Chronic Illnesses in Higher Education* and *Lived Experiences of Ableism in Academia: Strategies for Inclusion in Higher Education*. Her research interests relate to physical and material representations and metaphors, the generation of knowledge and, more generally, research methods and approaches to explore identity and body work. Her next book, *How to Make the Most of Your Research Journal*, will be published by Policy Press. She tweets as @ncjbrown @FibroIdentity @AbleismAcademia

Jennifer Leigh is a senior lecturer at the Centre for the Study of Higher Education, University of Kent.
j.s.leigh@kent.ac.uk
Jennifer joined the Centre for the Study of Higher Education full-time in 2013. She initially trained as a chemist, somatic movement therapist and yoga teacher before completing her doctorate in education at the University of Birmingham. She is a senior fellow of the Higher Education Academy. She edited a book for Routledge in 2019, *Conversations on Embodiment across Higher Education: Teaching, Practice and Research*. Together with Nicole Brown, she edited and contributed to *Ableism in Academia: Theorising Disabilities and Chronic Illnesses in Higher Education*, published by UCL Press in 2020. She is a founder member and vice chair of WISC (an international network for Women In Supramolecular Chemistry) and the only social scientist in the team. She has three

projects underway with WISC that bring embodied research approaches (and glitter) into the world of chemistry. Her next book, *The Boundaries of Qualitative Research: With Art, Education, Therapy and Science* will be published by Bristol University Press. Her research interests include embodiment, phenomenological and creative research methods, academic practice, academic development and ableism as well as aspects of teaching and learning in higher education. She tweets as @drschniff @suprachem.

SERIES EDITOR FOREWORD

The idea behind this book series is a simple one: to provide concise and accessible introductions to frequently used research methods and to current issues in research methodology. Books in the series have been written by experts in their fields with a brief to write about their subject for a broad audience.

The series has been developed through a partnership between Bloomsbury and the UK's National Centre for Research Methods (NCRM). The original 'what is' series sprang from the eponymous strand at NCRM's Research Methods Festivals, which ran for a number of years until 2018.

This relaunched series reflects changes in the research landscape, embracing research methods of innovation and interdisciplinarity. Methodological innovation is the order of the day, and the books provide updates to the latest developments whilst still maintaining an emphasis on accessibility to a wide audience. The format allows researchers who are new to a field to gain an insight into its key features, whilst also providing a useful update on recent developments for people who have had some prior acquaintance with it. All readers should find it helpful to be taken through the discussion of key terms, the history of how the method or methodological issue has developed and the assessment of the strengths and possible weaknesses of the approach through analysis of illustrative examples.

This book is devoted to the emerging field of embodied inquiry. In it, Jennifer Leigh and Nicole Brown provide an instructive account of how bodies are coming to be recognized as an important element in the research process. Attention to the significance of embodiment in the conduct of research has grown as research agendas have been extended to include diverse aspects of bodily influences and experiences. Nor is the growing interest in people's feelings and emotions confined to those of research participants; researchers' experiences have also been the subject of extensive reporting and debate as a consequence of reflexive engagement with questions about what it feels like to do research. It has proved challenging to undertake research into embodiment because the subject matter may be sensitive, requiring searching questions to be asked about bodies and emotions, and because time-honoured methods have sometimes proved inadequate to the task of collecting good quality data in this field. In response to these challenges, researchers adopting the embodied inquiry approach have drawn on a wide range of ideas from a variety of sources, both academic and practice-based, with remarkable imagination. This has resulted in the development of creative methods both singly and in combination as researchers endeavour to capture the elusive and multifaceted nature of embodiment. The diversity and fluidity of these methods are associated with interdisciplinary cross-pollination at the interface of the social sciences and arts and humanities, and Leigh and Brown wisely advise against seeking to locate researchers' practices in any neat and tidy analytical framework. Rather, they encourage adoption of the spirit of experimentation and creative engagement that characterizes the field.

The books in this series cannot provide information about their subject matter down to a fine level of detail, but they will equip readers with a powerful sense of why it deserves to be taken seriously and, it is hoped, with the enthusiasm to put that knowledge into practice.

Graham Crow and Mark Elliot

ACKNOWLEDGEMENTS

We would both like to thank Graham Crow for his invaluable support and both him and the publisher's anonymous reviewers for their detailed feedback on this manuscript. In addition, JL would like to acknowledge her ever-loving family and their acceptance of her appropriating the sofa as her office during the Covid-19 pandemic.

CHAPTER 1

What is Embodied Inquiry?

Introduction

Embodied Inquiry as a phrase is being used more frequently across research. Whereas once it might have been limited to fields and disciplines such as drama, physical education, dance or sport, this is no longer the case. But what does Embodied Inquiry mean? It is more than a development of qualitative research or an exact method that can be applied to a project, to make something pedestrian more exciting. Instead, it is an approach to the whole research process, or any part of the research process. Embodied Inquiry encourages us to use different methods and lenses in order to collect data and analyse embodied, lived experiences. It is not tied to any one theoretical approach, and yet, it is not atheoretical.

We both come from slightly different theoretical and practical understandings of embodiment. Whilst we are both from education, Nicole is a teacher, teacher educator and sociologist; Jennifer has a background in science and is a qualified yoga teacher and registered somatic movement therapist. As a consequence, Jennifer draws deeply on her training and experience in yoga and Authentic Movement, and a philosophical phenomenological perspective in order to inform her research practice and understanding of Embodied Inquiry. Nicole, by contrast, has long viewed her body as a tool, which she uses to model best practices within the context of initial teacher education.

Three Principles of Embodied Inquiry

Embodied Inquiry relies on and actively applies three foundational principles, which have been adapted from the principles of somatic movement (Leigh, 2012):

> The first principle sets out the 'What?' of Embodied Inquiry. Any Embodied Inquiry is part of an ongoing process of self. It asks for reflexivity, an exploration, attention to and non-judgemental awareness of self in addition to attention, exploration and non-judgemental awareness of others' experiences. Awareness of every movement and moment is a skill that can be learned and practised. It is likely to impact on life outside of the research study.
>
> The second principle answers 'Why?'. The starting point is that the body and mind are connected. By accessing the information, data and stories that bodies store, hold and tell, it is possible to reach deeper, emotional and authentic truths about lived experience than are accessed by more conventional research techniques.
>
> The 'How?' of an Embodied Inquiry is through conscious awareness, or the intention to incorporate this way of working into research. Not each Embodied Inquiry will look the same, nor will it necessarily feel the same for the researcher or participant. However, each Embodied Inquiry will either have explicitly defined these principles or at least implicitly adhere to them.

We will return to these in Chapter 7. In this book we will ask: What kind of research does Embodied Inquiry imply? What does it look like? What theoretical perspectives can be used? How might a researcher interested in Embodied Inquiry go about collecting, analysing and disseminating data? We will give an overview of what Embodied Inquiry might look like. We will introduce case studies of how we have used it in our own research to investigate academic identity and illness experiences and to capture embodied learning experiences with dancers. Drawing from our own research experience means that we are not using examples from all disciplines. We are aware that we do not refer to performance for example, even though this is a forum where Embodied Inquiry can be used. Instead, we offer practical guidance as to how Embodied Inquiry might inform, or be included in, research. We consider what it means in terms of designing research, collecting and analysing data, as well as the issues and challenges that can be associated with this type of work.

Embodiment and the Body in Focus

Conducting Embodied Inquiry does not mean that we have to take a particular theoretical or methodological perspective. There are many theoretical understandings and justifications for such work. This is best exemplified in Leigh (2019a), where fourteen academics from different theoretical backgrounds come into conversation about how their understandings of embodiment have impacted their teaching research and practice. All the work collected there could be termed Embodied Inquiry. Whilst all research should explicitly or implicitly be coherent with a theoretical frame, and though Embodied Inquiry needs to be conducted within a frame that allows for the possibility and importance of knowledge created from, by and within our bodies and minds, it does not mandate a particular theoretical approach. Particular methodologies and theoretical approaches are more naturally aligned to Embodied Inquiry. For example, in rhythmanalysis (Lefevbre, 2004; Lyon, 2019), and feminist and post-humanist theoretical perspectives (Barad, 2007), there can be an emphasis on embodied and sensory experiences. These interests in turn lend themselves to more creative or arts-based approaches, as Embodied Inquiry can draw on these as we will see in Chapter 5; however, it is not exclusively an arts-based approach. Research from this perspective may be researcher-orientated and internal such as practice by research (Trimingham, 2002) or practice as research (Spatz, 2020); it may explicitly focus on those practices or arts that look to increase self-awareness such as martial arts (Bowman, 2019), draw on a specific theorist such as Bourdieu (Pickard, 2007) or be concerned with complex issues such as identity in the developing world (Rajan-Rankin, 2018). Whatever the subject or framing, Embodied Inquiry will ask the researcher to be aware of their own experiences and positionality.

Using this Book

We all have bodies, feelings, emotions and experiences that affect the questions, we are interested in, the way in which we choose to approach finding out the answers to those questions and the patterns we see in the data we gather as a result. Embodied Inquiry foregrounds these questions of positionality and reflexivity in research. We have taken the decision to order this book much as we would approach an in-person workshop. After a quick overview of the history of Embodied Inquiry in both Western and non-Western contexts, we take a much more practical approach. We consider how you might design a project or study, and why you might choose to use multimodal and creative approaches to research in order to capture embodied experiences. We look at how you might analyse the types of data emerging from Embodied Inquiries, as well as the ethical considerations that are important to consider. Finally, we return to the three principles of Embodied Inquiry set out here, and look at what is, and what is not, Embodied Inquiry, before looking to the future.

As such, this book offers a critical and practical insight into Embodied Inquiry, the forms it might take, the value it might add to research and the considerations that need to be taken if Embodied Inquiry is employed as a research approach. We draw on our experiences as academics, movement therapists, educators and active researchers using embodied and creative methods in order to provide a succinct guide to and explanation of this innovative and exciting approach to research. Our perspective may seem Western-centric, because it reflects who we are, our backgrounds and what we have done. We have aimed this book at undergraduate and postgraduate students and researchers on a wide variety of courses and programmes, including sociology, education, disability studies, dance, performance, health studies, sport and exercise science, linguistics and drama: those who are interested in Embodied Inquiry generally, and those who are planning to undertake Embodied Inquiry. This approach speaks to all those interested in using qualitative research methods. It would also be useful for those on specific research methods courses for undergraduate or postgraduate students who are interested in creative and embodied approaches to research. It is not limited to social scientists, or arts-based researchers. It further supports those using practice as research as part of their postgraduate study at a Masters or Doctoral level in dance, drama, music or the arts.

The rest of this book is set out to consider why we might want to use Embodied Inquiry, and the benefits of this inclusive research approach. It is organized as follows:

Chapter 2 introduces a broad range of embodied explorations including discourses on the body, and movement practices that range from the therapeutic to the aesthetic. We draw examples from the East and the West and include psychotherapeutic movement-based approaches. Some may be familiar, whilst others may be new; all can be used to increase conscious self-awareness of the body, and the information that arises from the body.

Chapter 3 focuses on the foundational principles of Embodied Inquiry and practical aspects of how to design research for or to include aspects of Embodied Inquiry. We look at the types of questions and contexts where Embodied Inquiry may be applied – thus the research foci of the lived experience, the researcher's body in the field, bodies as communicators and the body in interaction. We show how Embodied Inquiry draws on phenomenology, hermeneutics, the cornerstones of human understanding and multimodality, which all underpin Embodied Inquiry. We conclude Chapter 3 with brief considerations on the role of reflexivity and the benefits of Embodied Inquiry.

Chapter 4 considers data within Embodied Inquiry and what role data collection, gathering and construction play. We outline how creative approaches to research can capture the multimodal aspects of Embodied Inquiry. Drawing on our own research projects, we present some different examples of creative research methods of the vast range available of arts-based practices, audio-visual modes of data capture and co-creation of knowledge and data.

Chapter 5 homes in to discuss how we might analyse the data produced within Embodied Inquiry. Again, we use practical examples to look at how different analytical approaches such as thematic, narrative and creative frames might add to the understanding of our research questions. Research in this way is an iterative process, as our reactions to our data will change as we change and are informed by our analytic journey. We conclude this chapter with an outline of how it is possible to ensure good quality within Embodied Inquiry.

In Chapter 6 we discuss issues and challenges of Embodied Inquiry, which include ownership of data when it is co-created, axiological issues that go beyond ethics processes such as how we can ensure our research is not exploitative, particularly when we are working with sensitive topics, and groups of participants who might be considered vulnerable due to their age, capacity or experience of trauma.

Chapter 7 considers the place of Embodied Inquiry, its validity and where it sits when determining rigour in research methods. We return to the three principles of Embodied Inquiry, and discuss what research might *not* be termed such. We look towards the future, and think about how Embodied Inquiry may be further advanced as a research approach.

CHAPTER 2

An Overview of Embodied Inquiry

Introduction

In this chapter we give an introduction to a broad range of embodied explorations and techniques. We include movement approaches from the East and the West, and an overview of psychotherapeutic movement approaches. Whilst an Eastern approach to the mind/body connection can be a foundation and framework for Embodied Inquiry, and offer useful methods to cultivate awareness of the self and the information that arises from the body, it is not the only approach that can be taken. In Chapter 3 we will discuss more conventional philosophical approaches such as phenomenology, and what we set out here can be seen as an alternative, or complementary, perspective. All these approaches will share (implicitly or explicitly) the three principles of Embodied Inquiry set out in Chapter 1.

Discourses on the Body

'Embodied' and 'embodiment' are contentious words (Sheets-Johnstone, 2015) that are understood and used in different ways. For example, from early classical sociology, the body was an 'absent presence' (Shilling, 2012, p. 21). The body was present as an entity central to the sociological imagination because humans are bodies, and being human is inextricably linked with embodiment and embodied experiences such as language or emotions. These sociologists would say that everything we do is embodied because we have meaty, fleshy, breathy bodies that carry us around the world. This would mean then that *all* research is Embodied Inquiry, because we are using our bodies in order to undertake it. However, the body was absent, in that it was not necessarily the primary focus of thinking and research. This does not automatically privilege or foreground what originates from the body. This sociological understanding of embodied, whilst pushing back against the idea that can be traced back through Descartes to Plato that the body is inferior to and separate from the mind (Plato, 2009), can still objectify the body. The body is seen as a thing, a living breathing container, through which we experience the world.

Other sociological theorists position the body as an explicit focus in relation to the concept of identity formation, recognizing the interconnected relationship between body and mind (Beck et al., 1994). The body is no longer seen as a mere vessel containing the human being. It shapes identity, and as such is a project involving development and improvement. In this context, the term 'embodied' is used to mean how we represent ourselves within and to the world around us, and how we might perform bodily modifications and transformations. This might be through our clothes; through 'disciplining' our body through exercise such as weightlifting and ballet; or through modifications such as tattoos, piercings or hairstyles so that we portray our identity by means of an outward expression of an inner sense. Through these expressions we show how we belong, or do not belong, to the society we find ourselves in. The body is described as a canvas, upon which individuals paint their personal identity. Bodies can be imperfect or broken (Oakley, 207). It is no longer enough to have a slim, symmetrical and beautiful body; we use surgical implants and medical solutions to allow our bodies to be super- and supra-human. The body is modified and moulded to fit specific purposes in society; it has become an entity of physical capital (Bourdieu, 2013/1984, 1986). Within social theory this corporeal realist perspective has come to be predominant. It places the body as a location for the transmission of societal and cultural norms and traditions, as a location for the lived experience and the recreation of society and culture (Shilling, 2012). The body is not experienced in isolation or in a vacuum of embodiment, but relates to and is related to the individual's identity (e.g. Charmaz, 1994, 1997; Charmaz et al., 2019; Ellingson, 2007, 2017). Many qualitative research methods and approaches advocate the importance of reflexivity and positionality. For example, ethnography asks those who engage with it to be reflexive. If we look to define ethnography, it may be defined as both a qualitative research process or method (one conducts an ethnography) and a product (the outcome of this process is an ethnography) whose aim is cultural interpretation. An ethnographic study is one that comes from ethnographic research. The ethnographer goes beyond reporting events and details of experience. An ethnography is a qualitative method where researchers completely immerse themselves in the lives, culture or situation they are studying. The idea of immersion immediately resonates with aspects of an Embodied Inquiry, as it plays to the thought that we are interested in recording and capturing the sensations and substance of an experience. Ethnographies are often lengthy studies, as they allow time for the researchers to become familiar with and accustomed to the culture or situation they are studying. Some examples of ethnography include traditional anthropological texts, but also work being done in marketing and user experience, such as conducting interviews to understand how the user relates to products or services.

Ethnography is associated with the Chicago School of Sociology, and work by Robert E. Park and Ernest W. Burgess and their students. The School used observations and conversations to gather data on the lived experiences of people within urban environments. The observers held themselves very much apart from those they were observing, and if we consider the differences in class, education and race this is hardly surprising. The School then looked to position their findings within the cultural and sociological context of the early twentieth century in order to generate knowledge on urban society.

Traditional anthropological ethnography also uses this approach to study cultures, and is now often considered to be problematic and a colonial way of working. The stereotypical image of this is captured in the idea of a white graduate student researching an Indigenous village. Many authors have written about the issues around traditional anthropology, for example, Martyn Hammersley:

These issues include: how ethnographers define the spatial and temporal boundaries of what they study; how they determine the context that is appropriate for understanding it; in what senses ethnography can be – or is – virtual rather than actual; the role of interviews as a data source; the relationship between ethnography and discourse analysis; the tempting parallel with imaginative writing; and, finally, whether ethnography should have, or can avoid having, political or practical commitments of some kind, beyond its aim of producing value-relevant knowledge. (Hammersley, 2006, p. 4)

A more 'blood and guts' approach to ethnography has been advocated by Loïc Wacquant (2006) in Body and soul: Notebooks of an apprentice boxer. Wacquant details in this book how he became engaged in boxing and trained to become a competition-level boxer. His work is ethnographic, and he is an active participant within his research, recording his own bodily experiences and sensations in his approach to his inquiry. That said, Wacquant, though bodily engaged as a participant, did not have the same lived experiences as his research subjects. He was separated from them by his race, education and, in part, his motivations to participate. Similar issues were raised by Alice Goffman (2014). Reflexivity and awareness of positionality cannot remove the distance between ourselves and our participants – however, it can highlight them, so that in our critical analysis, we do not overlook them.

Another advocate of paying attention to the sensory is Sarah Pink, who intentionally uses an embodied awareness to allow herself to capture and become aware of the sensory details of her research environment. These might be smells (such as the scent of freshly laundered clothes), sensations and the ways in which these play into our own memories, images and perceptions of a culture or situation (Pink, 2009). However, in order to carry out a sensory ethnography or Embodied Inquiry of any kind we need to be consciously self-aware of the information we get from our senses, our proprioception, our thoughts, feelings, images and emotions. We need to have that embodied self-awareness that we gain through experience of practices such as those outlined earlier, and take those experiences that often lie at an unconscious or unverbalized level up into consciousness and articulate them.

Other qualitative research methods and approaches, such as rhythmanalysis (see What is . . . Rhythmanalysis by Dawn Lyon (2019) for a comprehensive overview of the theoretical background and practical use of this research method) also highlight the need for an embodied approach and awareness. In rhythmanalysis, this can be so we can attend to the rhythms, eurhythms and arhythms of the space and people we are researching, using our own body as a research tool.

A History of Embodied Approaches

Eastern Perspectives

The value of all embodied approaches is that they challenge 'the dominant models of exercise, manipulation, and self-awareness that alienate people from their bodies' (Johnson, 1995, p. xiv). If we look at the history of using our bodies as a source of investigation and knowledge, then we can trace back how Embodied Inquiry has been used across the world. The novelty of it as a method or approach to research is more particular in a Western context than a global one. The traditional Eastern view of the body and mind is that they are inseparable aspects of the same human existence (Dychtwald, 1977). For example, we can consider yoga, which originated in India. Yoga as a philosophy and form has been known about for over 3000 years. Yoga is often translated as meaning union, yoking or communion, and is 'a poise of the soul which enables one to look at life in all its aspects evenly' (Gandhi, 1929, p. ix). Yoga is one of the six orthodox systems of Indian philosophy. One of the earliest yoga writings is a practical 'how to' manual called the *hatha yoga pradipika* (Vishnu-devanander, 1997) thought to date from the fifteenth century BCE, and compiled by Svatmarama. The core belief in yoga is that a body/mind split or duality as exemplified by Western culture is not a desired state of being, and, instead, practitioners work towards a cultivation of conscious awareness, or will. Wood (1959) talks of the will governing 'both mind and body . . . all things of the body and senses' (p. 20). Yoga is not a religion, nor is it easily classified as a philosophy, science or mythology. Yoga is more often described as an Art, or a Science, by senior practitioners (Iyengar, 1966), because it promotes the creation of knowledge within its proponents, as they actively learn more about themselves working towards their goals. The similarities to modern Embodied Inquiry are self-evident. Yoga can also be considered as something more resembling a Western form of psychotherapy, or 'a critique of culture' (Watts, 1961, p. 7), as it has at its heart the aim of personal liberation, a concept described as individuation or self-actualization. Traditionally, it is thought that by controlling the mind and developing mental discipline the student can reach a state of independence, liberty or freedom from the world around. This does not mean death, or unconsciousness, but an ability to live, and not be ruled by circumstances. This could be compared with the idea of developing an awareness, and reflexivity about the self. In the West, yoga is commonly thought of as only consisting of the third limb of the *astanga* system – of physical exercise. As such it is often found in gyms, and practised by those wanting to achieve a 'yoga body'. The many forms of yoga, and the Eastern philosophy that underpins it, can also be considered somatic practices and used for Embodied Inquiry, or as a training for embodied inquiries. However, just as the study of philosophy without the experiential awareness of the embodied self becomes a theoretical practice, likewise, the practice of yoga as only a means to fitness may not lead into an increased somatic awareness.

One aspect of Eastern movement forms that can result in Embodied Inquiry is that of stillness, or the 'moving into stillness in order to experience the truth of who you are' (Schiffmann, 1996, p. 4). The practice of being still is one aspect that separates yoga from physical education and other physical activities, and many martial arts, such as budo, also incorporate stillness or meditation in their practice (Stevens, 2001). By allowing awareness to focus in on bodies in a non-judgemental and accepting way, it is possible to release the negative perceptions that are held by the mind and the body. Increasing the direct experience of the body can be particularly effective in reducing self-objectification (Prichard and Tiggemann, 2008). Martial arts and yoga can be self-taught from books and videos, or taught within structured classes using imitative methods. Imitation as a means of learning body-based practices is discussed by Downey (2010) in relation to capoeira, a danced martial art. Capoeira is traditionally taught through imitation, minimal instruction, practice and exercises. It is experiential rather than theoretical. By watching, experimenting with and imitating a movement pattern or position, it is possible to integrate knowledge into action and understanding. However, in order for another to imitate, the teacher has to be embodied and present within their movements, and may also need to use touch, as 'an awareness of ourselves through skin contact of some sort does seem to be important for an on-going sense of self' (Westland, 2011, p. 21).

Zen comes at the 'problem' of reflection from a completely different perspective to that commonly expressed in educational literature discourse (Edwards and Nicoll, 2006), and has been described as the 'better part of reflective practice' (Tremmel, 1993, p. 442), meaning it is the most useful component. Zen is a practically accessible form of meditation, but hard to define purely in terms of language and thought. Again, it is experiential. Mindfulness (Bain, 1995), or the paying of attention to oneself and the world around, is a prerequisite, and can be utilized, as with other martial arts, to develop self-reflection. In relating the paradoxical qualities of Zen, Tremmel quotes Alan Watts (1957):

> Zen Buddhism is a way and a view of life which does not belong to any of the formal categories of modern Western thought. It is not religion or philosophy; it is not a psychology or a type of science. It is an example of what is known in India and China as a 'way of liberation', and is similar in this respect to Taoism, Vedanta and Yoga . . . A way of liberation can have no positive definition. (p. 3)

From our perspective of exploring Embodied Inquiry, the underlying commonality between these perspectives is the idea and philosophy that the body and mind are connected, and what comes from them is valuable and not weighted towards one perspective or another. They do not privilege the body over the mind (or vice versa) but, instead, they see them as inseparable. Such holistic outlooks are common in Indigenous perspectives, as part of a wider ontology, epistemology and axiology (Kara, 2018).

Western Movement Forms

In the West, somatic movement therapy, practices and bodywork approaches were being written about and practised in the first few decades of the last century. The term 'bodywork' implies an element of touch that may include, but is not limited to, massage or physical therapy: 'a variety of manipulative therapies' (Juhan, 1987, p. xix). They propose that by affecting the nervous system through tactile stimulation and movement it is possible to influence the organization of the mind and body, and the relationship we have with the environment around us: 'movement is the unifying bond between the mind and body, and sensations are the substance of that bond' (Juhan, 1987, p. xxv). Moving the body through different positions, and using it differently, can affect our emotional attitude (Cacioppo et al., 1993). There are many different types of bodywork. The bodywork practitioner would not necessarily work as an interventionist, but, rather, as a facilitator to aid a growing sense of self-awareness, a sense of the present embodied moment, and from that point a choice of alternatives. Such work could be useful to a researcher wanting to undertake Embodied Inquiry as a means of increasing conscious self-awareness, of processing the experiences of researching in this way, and as a starting point to investigate others' experiences. Many were developed in the early part of the nineteenth century in Western Europe and the United States; these include Gymnastik developed by Elsa Gindler (1885–1961), the Rosen Method (developed by Gindler's student Marion Rosen who also studied with a disciple of Carl Jung), Middendorf (developed by Ilse Middendorf), Alexander Technique (developed by F. M. Alexander), Feldenkrais (developed by Moshe Feldenkrais), Rolfing (developed by Ida Rolf), Aston Patterning (developed by Rolfing practitioner Judit Aston) and Eutony (developed by Gerda Alexander).

There is a long history of movement forms and practices that foreground the body-mind connection and embodied experience. Any or all of these could form the basis of Embodied Inquiry. The underlying commonality between these approaches is the idea and philosophy that the body and mind are connected, and what comes from them is valuable, and not weighted towards one perspective or another. They do not privilege the body over the mind (or vice versa) but, instead, they see them as inseparable. Such holistic outlooks are common in indigenous perspectives, as part of a wider ontology, epistemology and axiology (Kara, 2018). The practices are also often recommended for researchers to use for self-care (Ellingson, 2017), a topic we return to in Chapter 6.

Psychotherapeutic and Movement-Based Practices

Many embodied practices explicitly or implicitly cross the boundary into psychotherapeutic techniques. Unlike traditional Eastern movement forms such as yoga or martial arts, they claim therapeutic intent or affect as a direct result of the practitioner's intervention. The idea of the practitioner's thought and will shaping the process has similarities to Edmund Husserl's approach to phenomenology where 'through intentionality we will our entire world into being and give it shape' (Zuesse, 1985, p. 53). Indeed, Thorburn states that 'the essence of an experience is its intentionality: the meaning of events, the meaning of embodied action including kinaesthetic awareness of one's movements and the importance of sensations as they are experienced by the body' (and, p. 265). This resonance between movement and phenomenology has implications for methodological choices, which we will look at in more detail in Chapter 3. Mauri Merleau-Ponty articulated a concept of lived space, where, rather than being bound by reason/emotion mind/body dichotomies, the subject's experience is referenced through movement and language (Thorburn, and).

Dance Movement Therapy originated from the work of Rudolf Von Laban. His exploration of the emotional and psychological dimensions of movement patterns was brought to the United States by Irmgard Bartenieff (1900–81). She trained with Laban in Berlin, in the first few years of his school. Laban was a contemporary of Elsa Gindler, Frederick Alexander, Emile Jacques-Dalcroze and Sigmund Freud amongst others. His work resulted from the study of martial arts, and was applied to dancers. Laban developed Labanotation, a way in which to record the movements of dancers and to choreograph. His trainings emphasized 'exploring your own capacities in the movement' (Rubenfeld, 1977, p. 11), and he later developed dance within the English Public School system. Bartenieff trained in physical therapy and worked with children rehabilitating from polio. She introduced dance and dance rhythm to bedridden children, and liaised with their psychiatrists and art therapists to work 'on the mental problems as well as the physical' (Rubenfeld, 1977, p. 11). She went on to work with patients suffering from mental illness as a dance movement therapist and use how movement influences the state of mind. In contrast to the movement practices outlined earlier, dance movement therapy is regulated along with other psychotherapeutic techniques, and has its own national professional bodies (e.g. association for dance movement psychotherapy in the UK https://admp.org.uk/, and the American Dance Therapy Association https://adta.org/). Its focus on the psychotherapeutic aspects of movement would make it a useful approach for research that centres on those who have suffered trauma.

Integrative Bodywork and Movement Therapy was developed by Linda Hartley, using the principles of Body-Mind-Centering® (BMC®) as developed by Bonnie Bainbridge-Cohen in the United States in the 1970s. Bainbridge-Cohen was an occupational therapist and trained dancer. She trained as a physical therapist with Babette Bobath, who developed a revolutionary approach to working with cerebral palsy. Bainbridge-Cohen began to use ideas of effortlessness, and the lengthening rather than the stretching of muscles, taking inspiration from modern dancer Erik Hawkins, who used Japanese aesthetics, Greek civilization and Zen Buddhism in his work. She began to work privately, using the developmental work with dancers and adults interested in movement. She included experiential anatomy – the lived and experienced exploration of the body. The classes and groups that she led began with explorations of the musculo-skeletal structure, then grew to include the organs and the nature of the other tissues within the body, including the nervous system and the endocrine glands, the bodily fluids (blood, lymph, cerebrospinal fluid, synovial fluid, tissue and cellular fluids) and also the perceptual movement process including the mouth, hands, eyes, nose and skin. She began to notice that the quality of movement of each was very different, depending on what the person was putting in his mind, and where he initiated movement from. Her students and trainee teachers began to 'perceive the different mind-states and feelings which emerged depending on the place of initiation . . . as we change from one body area to another, the mind of the room changes' (Bainbridge-Cohen, 1993, p. 10). Hartley (2004) developed her own framework of therapy and training (accredited by the International Somatic Movement Education Therapy Association (ISMETA, nd)), integrating elements of dance movement therapy and transpersonal psychotherapy of psychosynthesis and process-orientated psychology. Hartley's identification of the ways in which 'somatic work does touch upon deep emotional and psychological processes' (2004, p. 28) and use of Authentic Movement developed her graduates' 'Therapeutic Presence', where 'the therapist's perceptions can be offered to a client, but owned for what they are – her own interpretations, judgements and projections' (Hartley, 2004, p. 30). In Integrative Bodywork and Movement Therapy, great importance is placed on the practitioner or therapist's role in reflecting back to the client her own experience of the body, and the intention of the practitioner's touch. Hartley's work has greatly influenced this book. Body-Mind-Centering® and Integrative Bodywork and Movement Therapy are both holistic approaches, combining educational and therapeutic techniques that can be used exploratively as well as therapeutically. As such, they offer a great deal of versatility within Embodied Inquiry.

Authentic Movement is a ritualized form of movement or dance therapy created by Mary Starks Whitehouse (1911–79). It focuses on the relationship between a mover and a witness, and gives equal weight to both the moving process and the verbal sharing of the mover's and witness's experiences of the movement (Hartley, 2004). Because of the ritual of the form, it is challenging to describe it without the words becoming jargonistic, as is the case with yoga and its Sanskrit vocabulary. At its simplest, Authentic Movement involves moving from felt internal impulses, and nurturing the feelings and emotions that are released. According to Dance Movement Therapists, Authentic Movement offers a powerful form within which the depths of the inner psyche can speak directly through the body:

> making use of spontaneous body movement that arose from inner kinaesthetic sensations, individuals recognised the symbiotic nature of their communications which then opened the door to self-awareness and possible change. (Chaiklin, 2009, p. 7)

It is claimed that the discipline of bringing the bodily experience into language works to heal the split that language can cause in the experience of the self (Chaiklin, 2009), which is why it can be so valuable as we learn to articulate our experience and awareness for Embodied Inquiry. We will look at the process of transcription as one element of this in Chapter 5. Authentic Movement offers a holding space, a feminine container, and a 'practice of embodied awareness that goes beyond therapy' (Hartley, 2004, p. 56). The differentiation of movement originating from the unconscious rather than the conscious was part of Whitehouse's practice of embodying Jung's process of active imagination. She separated movements that were intentional, unintentional and those that came from within the self, that is, the sense of 'I am moving', 'I am being moved' and an embodiment of both experiences. She believed that by working with the unconscious self, we are able to access the emotional core of our complexes. Additionally to this, it is possible to move between personal, transpersonal and collective impulses.

Additional evolutions of the discipline of Authentic Movement were developed by Janet Adler, among others. Whereas Whitehouse focused on the direct experience of the mover (Whitehouse, 1995), and the process of active imagination in movement, Adler addressed the direct experience of both mover and witness (Hartley, 2004). Authentic Movement can be practised in its ground form, with one mover and a witness. It is the role of the witness to create the witness circle, a safe, held space in which the mover moves with eyes closed, following internal impulses. The shutting of the eyes enables the mover to give her full attention to what she senses internally and imagines. The form and expression of the inner story is allowed to unfold, until, usually after a mutually agreed time, the witness signals the end of the movement session by the ringing of a bell or other signal. Both the mover and the witness attend to their own experiences whilst the mover moves; however, it is the role of the witness to contain the experience by marking the time boundary. The experiences are anchored into the consciousness by recalling it to the witness, or recording it through artwork or writing. The witness then offers her personal responses to the mover, helping to bring unconscious material into consciousness, and integrating the unconscious with the conscious. According to the Jungian process of active imagination, the final stage of integration occurs without great effort and resistance, and from there it is possible to make changes in everyday life (Adler, 2002). If we liken this process to that of researcher and researched, we can see that the researcher (witness) holds the boundary and safeguards the researched (mover), and it is the process of articulating the experience that allows it to be processed.

Authentic Movement is a discipline and not psychotherapy, although it can effect therapeutic changes. It may be used within a therapeutic practice, but it is recommended that it is done so only by practitioners with a therapeutic training. Some practise Authentic

Movement as a tool towards mindful living, as a contemplative tool to aid spiritual growth or as a creative resource. The form was taught to Jennifer as part of the Integrative Bodywork and Movement Therapy training in order to learn the skills of therapeutic presence, an embracing attitude in which speech is clear, and there is a holistic, non-judgemental acceptance of others. It has been used explicitly as a research tool by Jane Bacon (2010), by Jennifer in a study exploring academic identity (Leigh, 2019b), and by Jennifer and Nicole in work with undergraduate students (Petsilas et al., 2019a, b). These last two studies are used as case studies in Chapter 3.

Similar ideas about the importance of embodied processes and movement were being developed at this time (1960s onwards) within the world of drama and performance with the work of Grotowski and the like. Although this type of exploratory movement and bodywork may be considered different and new by some,

> for yoga to have developed, somebody somewhere must have had the awareness that one could initiate from all of the various organs. And in the martial arts, people speak of points or centers, and I think it must be internal, organic energy they're talking about. I don't feel what we're doing is new; what I feel we're offering is some kind of translation into the Western vocabulary. (Bainbridge-Cohen, 1993, p. 11)

In therapeutic movement approaches, as described briefly here, the psychological process of the client is emphasized, alongside experiential exploration of anatomy and movement patterns. As such, there is a need for the client to be held in an unconditional and positive regard. In addition, the practitioner needs to be aware of the psychological and emotional processes that may be touched through somatic bodywork, whether they are addressed specifically or not. This approach is termed Person, or Client-Centred (Rogers, 1967). It is very easy to make the parallel here between researcher and practitioner, and researched and client. If, by using Embodied Inquiry, we are touching our own and our participants' emotional and embodied experiences, we need to be conscious about holding space for them.[1]

---

[1] The idea of the boundary between therapy and research is explored further in the forthcoming book, Leigh, J. (2023) *Boundaries of research: Between qualitative research, art, education, therapy, and science. To be published by Bristol University Press.*

Chapter Summary

This chapter has given a brief overview of the history of embodied inquiry, including:

- different sociological understandings of the body
- ethnographic research approaches that centre the body and its experiences
- Eastern perspectives such as yoga, martial arts and Zen
- Western movement forms that originated from the early 1900s
- psychotherapeutic and movement-based practices, including Dance Movement Therapy, Body-Mind-Centering© and Authentic Movement

CHAPTER 3

Designing for Embodied Inquiry

Introduction

In this chapter we expand on what Embodied Inquiry is and what an attention to embodiment can bring to research. Whilst Embodied Inquiry can use a multitude of theoretical lenses and frames as highlighted in Chapters 1 and 2, this chapter looks at which research questions may be particularly conducive to Embodied Inquiry and how a research project might be designed as Embodied Inquiry. We give examples of different research phases, types of research questions and the ways in which a researcher may set out to find the answers to those research questions. This chapter includes a brief introduction to the importance of philosophical outlooks, which will impact the kind of Embodied Inquiry a researcher is embarking on. We conclude this chapter with some key considerations relating to the researcher's positionality within Embodied Inquiry.

Research Focus for Embodied Inquiry

Before discussing the detailed design of Embodied Inquiry, we consider which kinds of research questions would be best answered through Embodied Inquiry. The design for Embodied Inquiry depends initially on the nature of the research focus, but more specifically on the particular research question within that

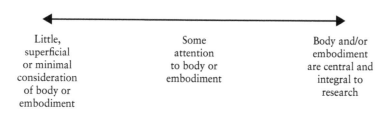

| Little,
superficial
or minimal
consideration
of body or
embodiment | Some
attention
to body or
embodiment | Body and/or
embodiment
are central and
integral to
research |

FIGURE 3.1 *Continuum of Embodied Inquiry.*

broader focus. Generally, Embodied Inquiry seeks to account for and focus on something that is frequently: bodily and embodied experiences. As with every research process, Embodied Inquiry can also be perceived as a continuum where the researchers consider embodiment only minimally or superficially on the one end and may be paying attention to the body if somewhere on the continuum, whereas on the other end of the spectrum, embodiment and the body are the central concern (Figure 3.1).

Following but extending Ellingson (2017), we offer a typology of four kinds of research foci that lend themselves to designing specifically for Embodied Inquiry: (a) lived experiences, (b) the researcher's body in the field, (c) the body as a communicator and (d) the body in interaction. The typology presented here shows how Embodied Inquiry is concerned with experiences and functions that are embodied and bodily, but it also highlights that the approach to Embodied Inquiry must be holistic in that, for example, the above research foci cannot be entirely separated from one another, but also overlap and interrelate. Typologies in their nature are vulnerable to ambiguity and many of the examples provided within the specific sections that follow may fit within the context of two or three of the categories. The overlaps and interrelation of the categories become particularly evident in Chapter 4, where we present case studies of our own research projects in detail. The continuum of Embodied Inquiry is crucial in providing order and clarity, and in identifying the role and prominence embodiment and the body are to have in an entire project.

The Lived Experience

Research questions that relate to the participants' lived experiences are a prime example for Embodied Inquiry. The Embodied Inquiry here offers insights that are different from the ones gained through interviewing or narrative approaches. Whilst interview and narrative methods allow for the researcher to explore what participants think and how they make sense of their lived experiences, Embodied Inquiry seeks to get close to, understand and to an extent recreate the participants' lived experiences. Embodied Inquiries into lived experiences can involve participants' health concerns (Bates, 2019). Explorations of the lived experience can also relate to everyday tasks, such as the process of doing laundry (Pink, 2015) or sports and leisure activities (Allen-Collinson and Owton, 2015; Faulkner, 2018). The body as a project may provide insights into the lived experiences of identity work (Inckle, 2009; Weiss, 2013), as would the consideration of the intersectionality of bodies (Ellingson, 2017). The human body is a complex system of sensory experiences, which is often limited to the five senses of touch, sight, taste, smell and sound (Pink, 2015; Eccleston, 2016). If, however, we allow for an interpretation of the sensorium that is functionalist but grounded in existential psychology, structuralism and phenomenology (Eccleston, 2016), we can extend the sensorium to include proprioceptive and interoceptive domains. Proprioception is the experience of space and positionality and as such includes balance and movement. Interoception relates to the conscious and unconscious internal workings and states of the body and therefore includes bodily functions like pain, fatigue, itch. An exploration of the sensorium therefore may focus on the experience of balance through an investigation into falling or dizziness (Yardley, 1999), or it may relate to experiences of breathing, hiccupping, sneezing (Virtbauer, 2016) and the like.

The Researcher's Body in the Field

Being in the field, engaging with others, being immersed in particular contexts and environments requires the researcher to be prepared to experience and live what is new, unexplored and not understood at this point. The researcher therefore experiences emotional responses such as wonder, amazement, fright and disgust, which in turn translate into bodily and embodied expressions. However, instead of merely recognizing the researcher's self in personal notes and comments, research questions may focus on the researcher's body in the field. Embodied Inquiry recognizes the researcher's body as a tool for inquiry, which in turn makes it the subject of the project. Anthropological and ethnographical research in particular have focused on the researcher's learning processes (Csordas 1994, 2002; Jordan, 2001; Bodenhorn, 2016; Halstead, 2016). Embodied Inquiry may also explore the transformation researchers experience in and through being involved in their research, not merely through engaging with others but also through reflecting on how their engagement with others impacts them (Lewis, 2017; Attia and Edge, 2017). The researcher's body may also be at the centre of projects applying rhythmanalysis (Lyon, 2019; Lefebvre, 2004). In Lefebvre's intention, rhythmanalysis is a form of inquiry that emphasizes the researcher's embodied experience of rhythms and patterns in the lifeworld, through which the researcher can explore social life and provide insights into how people engage in social worlds. The researcher's body in the field becomes particularly central in autoethnography and autoethnographic explorations (van den Scott, 2018; McMahon and Thompson, 2011; Ettorre, 2010).

The Body as a Communicator

Interviews are often treated as disembodied or unembodied events. In truth, any interaction between a participant and a researcher is an opportunity for two bodies interconnecting and interacting with one another. Embodied Inquiry therefore may focus on the body as a communicative and expressive tool constructing new knowledge and data. In addition to the words that are spoken, interactions between researchers and participants are considered in relation to their nonverbal communication. Gestures, facial expressions and movements count as data sets that are important complements to the spoken word (Heath, 2002; Alibali and Nathan, 2012). The body as a communicator is also central in research into tattoo culture (Leader, 2015, 2016) and practices within the hair and beauty industry (McCabe et al., 2017; Flores, 2016; Crawford Sheare, 2008), and within the context of fashion (Frith and Gleeson, 2004; Thapan, 2004). The body communicates and is used to listen (Back, 2007), express emotions, communicate ideas and represent opinions. The body as a communicator is particularly problematized in works by Chadwick (2017) and Sandelowski

(1994), for example. These research articles report specifically on methodological issues around interview transcriptions and thereby highlight the many forms and facets of bodily communications we encounter in research processes.

The Body in Interaction

Our reality is socially constructed and interdependent and therefore even isolated bodily events such as sneezing or coughing in public (particularly relevant in relation to the Covid-19 Pandemic) are organized around social conventions and do not actually occur in isolation. Embodied Inquiry may focus on investigating such behaviours in order to offer insights into patterns of interactions and factors influencing individuals' behaviours. As a consequence, Embodied Inquiry allows researchers to theorize and conceptualize social realities (Vannini, 2016). Therefore, Embodied Inquiry that considers the body in interaction and as a social entity demands of researchers an awareness of interactional practices and social settings (Gibson and Vom Lehn, 2020) as well as of their personal positioning, movements, actions and reactions (Vannini, 2016). The body in interaction as a research focus is, however, not limited to interactions with other bodies, but may also relate to how bodies act and interact within the time-space continuum (Lyon, 2016; Brown and Morgan, 2021). Further lines of inquiry relating to the body in interaction could be related to movement-orientated therapy, such as dance movement therapy which expressly considers how movement influences the state of mind:

> I sometimes tell people . . . to put their arms towards the ceiling and say 'I'm depressed' . . . it's a fun way of demonstrating how movement affects feeling, and feelings affect movement. (Leder, 1990, p. 154)

For most people, raising their arms and opening out the chest lightens their mood, which is at odds with feeling depressed, a feeling more associated with hunched, slumped or defeated postures (Hartley 1989; Fogel 2009). However, it must be noted that a soldier indicating surrender might do so by raising his arms, thus feeling deflated. In addition to capturing movements, an Embodied

Inquiry can consider how people feel about movements they make or see others making, adding an additional layer and potential for analysis.

Foundations of Embodied Inquiry

As we have outlined so far, Embodied Inquiry is a form of research that puts the body into the centre of the investigation. The typology presented earlier shows that this may be done in many different forms. However, once we consider more closely the many research projects dealing with the body and embodiment, we notice a theoretical foundation that is common to them all: namely, the focus on interpretations of experiences, thus the connection with phenomenology and hermeneutics.

Phenomenology

On its foundational level, phenomenology is an approach to study experience. However, phenomenological traditions have developed throughout time, and there is not one singular, unified definition of what phenomenology is or looks like. Phenomenology is most deeply associated with Edmund Husserl (1927) who proposed a phenomenology that looks to identify the core or essence of an experience and phenomenon. To achieve this, Husserl advocated that researchers become aware of their own thoughts and biases and try to block or blank those out, so that they cannot influence the existing investigation. The complexity of phenomenology becomes evident when we consider phenomenology as understood by Martin Heidegger, who was Husserl's student. In Heidegger's (1996/1953) understanding, human being-in-the-world and human self cannot be separated from other people and the interactions with these others. Heidegger believed that any being is a person in context and an intersubjective being. If for Husserl the phenomenon was there and given, for Heidegger a phenomenon existed as part of interpretational or relational experience. This relational experience was further developed by Merleau-Ponty (2005/1962), who emphasized embodiedness and bodily being. In Merleau-Ponty's terms humans are body-subjects whose being is holistic, engaged in looking at the world, and where the body is not an object but a means to communicate. In addition to these three interpretations of phenomenology, there are many other slightly distinct traditions (see Smith et al., 2012 and Dahlberg et al., 2007 for more details). For the purpose of Embodied Inquiry, we take from phenomenology the emphasis we place on experience and embodiment, that as humans we do not exist in a vacuum but are located and set in the world as relational and contextual beings and that our being-in-the-world is personal to us, as we interpret our experiences.

Hermeneutics

The second strand feeding into Embodied Inquiry stems from hermeneutics, which is the theory of interpretation. In the previous section, we introduced Heidegger (1996/1953), for whom understanding and experience were interpretational and relational. The step for Embodied Inquiry to draw on hermeneutics is therefore a logical consequence. Again, as is the case with so many philosophies and traditions, definitions are not as clear-cut as we may want them to be because researchers and scholars mould the pure forms to fit their purposes and aims. In its basic principle, hermeneutics refers to the fact that in order to communicate or understand as humans we interpret individual elements and combine them to make sense of the entirety (Zimmermann, 2015). Within this context, hermeneutic scholars acknowledge that interpretation is just that, an interpretation, which does not necessarily have to be correct, and that texts may well be misunderstood, if the interpreter is not aware of the contextual details of a text or its producer (Gadamer, 2006/1975; Bingham, 2010). In order to overcome these misinterpretations and inaccuracies, hermeneutic scholars refer to the 'hermeneutic circle'. The hermeneutic circle forms a substantial part of hermeneutic theory and is the element that Embodied Inquiry takes from hermeneutics. The hermeneutic circle describes how individual parts and the whole are interrelated, which provides the impetus for interpretations to flow from the details and the specific to the general and the bigger picture and back to the details and particularities. The hermeneutic circle therefore grants the researcher freedom to move backwards and forwards during the interpretative process. Indeed, as we will see in Chapter 5, quality in Embodied Inquiry can be guaranteed only if analysis is iterative and moves fluidly between different aspects of interpretation and elements of data. However, in Embodied Inquiry we like to think about the hermeneutic circle as a spiral rather than an unbroken circle, as the image of a circle implies no beginning or end, whereas the image of a spiral evokes the connotation of delving deeper and deeper into matters and phenomena. If, for example, a participant making sense of their data or the researcher making sense of participants' data represents a first level of that hermeneutic spiral, then the researcher and participant together making sense of the participant making sense of the data represents a second, much deeper interpretative level in the hermeneutic spiral.

Cornerstones of Human Understanding and Communication

In addition to the philosophical groundings in phenomenology and hermeneutics, Embodied Inquiry builds on the fact that communication is more than verbal expression and that human understanding is complex, which is founded on three basic observations (Brown, 2019b, 2020): (a) human understanding is embodied (Finlay, 2015); (b) language is insufficient and inexact (Scarry, 1985; Sontag, 2003); and (c) communication and human understanding are metaphorical (Lakoff and Johnson, 2003). These three observations build the cornerstones for the framework underpinning Embodied Inquiry, which is based on multimodality anchored in phenomenology and hermeneutics.

Human Understanding is Embodied

This tenet is best exemplified in the behaviours and developments of babies and toddlers, who explore their surroundings in ways that are physical and embodied (Hartley, 1989). How we interact and engage with the world as infants can affect how we later move through and form relationships within it (Bainbridge-Cohen, 1993). According to Piaget (1953/2011), babies and toddlers of up to eighteen to twenty-four months of age experience a sensorimotor phase as part of their cognitive development. This phase is introduced through the body's reflexes, of which the sucking reflex is the most pronounced. Babies will then gradually develop sucking habits as well as vision and hearing. However, the sucking reflex and habits provide the grounding through which babies initially experience their being-in-the-world. This is the time when children learn through looking and hearing, but more often through touching, licking and sucking. Although Piaget's description of cognitive development stages should not be viewed uncritically, the fact remains that the earliest forms of experiences are embodied and physical (Montagu, 1971), as babies are picked up, cuddled and held, and therefore their bodies are moved and swayed (Finlay, 2015).

Language is Insufficient and Inexact

There are experiences in life, for which we do not have exact descriptions or words. To demonstrate this, we would like you to take part in a short exercise:

> Close your eyes.
> Think of a headache.
> And try to describe that headache.

You may have been thinking of 'splitting', 'pounding', 'stabbing', 'nagging', 'nauseating' or you may have thought about how some headaches are located more centrally on your forehead, whereas others are at the back of the head, with others focused on your temples. Not every headache is the same. The headache from a migraine feels drastically different from the headache we feel coming on in periods of anxiety, the headache we get just before we develop a high fever or the headache that is a symptom and result of a hangover.

As this little thought experiment shows, some descriptions are helpful, but they are not sufficient in fully explaining the experience we are going through. In fact, pain is a particularly difficult experience to explain, describe and communicate (Scarry, 1985; Sontag, 2003) because in most cases we cannot see any signs of pain and therefore struggle to reconcile a face in agony with what we are seeing, which is nothing. We rely on language to convey the experience of pain. Language is a vital part of Embodied Inquiry. Movement underlies language, and language arises from our embodied experience (Sheets-Johnstone, 2009).

Communication and Human Understanding are Metaphorical

As a result of the fact that human understanding is embodied and that language is not precise enough, our communication and understanding are largely metaphorical (Lakoff and Johnson, 2003). Everyday phrases like 'I feel blue' or 'he feels on top of the world' are indicators of how much we rely on expressions through metaphors. Similarly, we sometimes rely entirely on gestures like 'thumbs up' or emoticons that express everything we would like to say in that particular point in time. This final example also highlights what is often quoted in educational contexts, namely that only 40 per cent of all human communication is in fact verbal, and the remaining 60 per cent is, indeed, nonverbal, in the forms of eye contact, facial expressions, gestures, postures and the like (Birdwhistell, 1970, 1974).

Multimodality

As a consequence of the three tenets that human understanding is embodied, that language is insufficient and inexact and that communication and human understanding are metaphorical, Embodied Inquiry draws on multimodality. Although 'multimodal' and 'multimodality' are commonly used in research contexts, the precise meaning is somewhat difficult to grasp and requires deeper thought. The compound consists of the two elements 'multi' and 'modes' or 'modality'. Modes or modality describe the 'means for making meaning' – thus all the different elements humans have at their disposal to express and make meaning. Multimodality therefore refers to 'multiple means of making meaning'. The real concern of multimodality lies with the understanding that many modes, thus the different means and elements for making meaning, appear together and not in separation from one another. For example, we use images with written text or we use gestures in addition to the spoken word to convey particularities and details.

Multimodality therefore is not merely the consideration of different elements for making meaning. At its core lies the understanding that different elements of making meaning cannot be separated out from one another, that they need to be considered holistically and that the event of communication and expression is a 'multimodal whole' rather than a composite of separate entities or units (Jewitt et al., 2016). Multimodal research therefore consists of and includes specific characteristics. Embodied Inquiry does not seek to replicate multimodal research. Instead, Embodied Inquiry engages with multimodality and takes from it its interest in and openness to 'modes', often leaving the choices regarding forms of communication to participants (see also Chapter 4).

Approaching Embodied Inquiry

The previous sections highlighted many theoretical foundations of Embodied Inquiry, which need to be thoroughly understood. Within that broad framework of thought the key element in Embodied Inquiry is the focus on bodily and embodied experiences. Beyond that, however, Embodied Inquiry is very flexible and open and does not prescribe one particular way of carrying out research, as is evidenced in the different examples mentioned in the previous section.

Therefore, once researchers have decided to embark on an Embodied Inquiry, they will need to consider embodiment and the role of the researcher's and participants' bodies across the different stages of the research to best fit the aims and purposes of the research. To this end, they should reflect on their research question and how it fits into the typology described earlier before considering what it is that they are trying to achieve with their research. In order to identify where on the continuum of Embodied Inquiry they will position themselves and how therefore they will design their research project, they need to ask themselves what it is they want to achieve with their work. Do they want to find out about a particular experience? Or are they interested in the role of the researcher? Are they comfortable with sharing their experiences as a researcher? Will they consider how the bodies of the researcher and participants interact? Do they want to account for bodily experiences as part of the analytical process? How will findings be disseminated? What is the purpose of sharing the findings? These questions are meant to be food for thought regarding what kind of Embodied Inquiry a researcher may want to embark upon. In practice, there will again be overlaps and connections, as is exemplified in the case studies presented in Chapter 4.

Some of these questions relate to fundamental research principles and are ontological and epistemological in nature. Being very conscious and transparent about what researchers consider reality, truth and knowledge, and how these realities, truths and knowledges can be accessed, provides the grounding for designing a successful Embodied Inquiry. For example, if someone believes that they would like to get as close as possible to a phenomenon or experience, they may want to include an attention to embodiment within data collection. If, however, disseminating findings in a way that allows individuals to engage or be affected is central to the research, then attending to embodiment in analysis and dissemination is crucial.

Approaches to research will and should differ if a researcher emphasizes original contributions to a field or if they seek to account for social justice and activism 'to make life better for a person, or a group of persons' (Denzin, 2016, p. 42). As a result of that specific way of investigating, there are many different methods and lenses available for collecting and analysing data within Embodied Inquiry. We would like to reiterate here what we emphasized in Chapters 1 and 2 that Embodied Inquiry encourages that multitude of methods and approaches, not because it is atheoretical, but because it requires and encourages an appropriate, well-thought-through design in response to specific questions and research foci.

Benefits of Embodied Inquiry

Conducting Embodied Inquiry and bringing elements of embodiment into the research process also allow for inclusive research practices. The basis of inclusivity lies in challenging the hierarchical Cartesian duality and power relation of mind over body. Exemplifying the far-reaching impact of such a duality, Drew Leder (1990) links the Cartesian duality to the domination of men over women as follows:

> women have consistently been associated with the bodily sphere. They have been linked with nature, sexuality and the passions,

whereas men have been identified with the rational mind. This equation implicitly legitimizes structures of domination. (Leder, 1990, p. 154)

This comparison with hierarchies of oppression could also be applied to the oppressions of class, race, disability and the like. One aspect is identified with the body, the other (the oppressor) with the mind, and the Cartesian view of seeing an inferior, external 'other' that is mindless and in need of control justifies subjugation. Phenomenology can be used as a tool to logically refute or criticize a dualist approach. However, this argument, made without experiential knowledge and understanding, can become yet another discourse that once again panders to the rational mind, and ignores not only the body but also the reality of an embodied self. Perceiving and understanding the body-mind as a whole and unified thing, rather than a separated split body and mind, is a different ontological standpoint. By centring Embodied Inquiry, it is possible to challenge oppressive structures that would silence the voices of marginalized people, and allow those who find themselves ignored to have a voice. Embodied Inquiry does not automatically or naturally engage bodies that are marginalized and sidelined, but with its critical-reflexive focus it offers an opportunity to reconsider positions of power, hierarchy and control and to see who is absent from a discourse. In this context, wider philosophical standpoints as presented in Chapter 2 are particularly helpful in foregrounding individual, embodied experiences.

Through centring embodied experiences of the researcher, and/ or the researched at the development, data collection, analytic or dissemination stages of a research project, a reflexive approach is centred. One way to develop embodied awareness and reflexivity is through the use of 'positive practices' such as those outlined in Chapter 2. However, we need to approach such practices with a clarity of what they will do, and what our intention is in using them this way. Such 'positive practices' including yoga, martial arts and some forms of dance or meditation are deemed to be optional by Leder (1990), only being sought out by those actively seeking them. He continues by giving the opinion that although there are Western equivalents to these forms that increase relaxation, coordination, ecstasy and concentration, in general, Western philosophical and religious traditions take a negative view towards the body and do not place an emphasis on cultivating it. If positive body affirming and awareness practices are not habitually part of life, then awareness of the body is remembered mostly when it is in pain, tired, lustful, diseased or dying. If we do not experience our body positively, then it is more likely that we subject it to abuse and neglect that leads to illness and physical decline, thus further perpetuating the cycle (Fogel, 2009; Leder, 1990).

If we think about developing the ability to be reflexive, reflexivity is not the same as reflective practice, though the two are linked (Leigh and Bailey, 2013). Being reflexive in research is a key benefit of an Embodied Inquiry. Reflexivity is a benefit to any type of research, and at any part of the research process, as it requires us as researchers to be aware of who we are, what we are doing and why we are doing it. It is closely linked to ideas of positionality, in that in order to be aware of our positionality, we need to be reflexive. These are connected, iterative processes in that in order to be reflexive, we need to be consciously self-aware, and in order to be consciously self-aware, we need to reflect on who we are and what our assumptions are. Such skills are useful not only within an Embodied Inquiry but also for any type of research. Whilst some delineate 'soft' and 'hard' methods and approaches, it can be argued that 'soft' methods are not easy, but more subtle, and that 'hard' denotes inflexibility not strength (Payne and Payne, 2004). In both 'soft' science and 'hard' science we can be reflexive about our choices to pursue one line of inquiry over another, to take one approach over another. Similarly, we can be aware of our positionality when we choose to study one research question over another (why *this* cancer, why *this* type of community?) and this will have the benefit of deepening our awareness of and engagement with our research. Reflexivity and positionality go beyond a surface-level recognition of characteristics of ourselves as individuals and members of society. Embodied Inquiry is a way of centring and foregrounding these aspects of the research process, and also provides a means of learning and practising the skills that are needed to do this.

If we return to Authentic Movement that we discussed in Chapter 2, and the idea of witnessing, developing witness skills is something that is of immense use to the researcher who wants to become reflexive. An experienced witness can observe, track and recall movement, sensations, thoughts, emotions and images of themselves and others. A challenge of traditional ethnography is the tension between participating and note-taking – a criticism of audio-visual recording is the distance created between the image and the experience.

When beginning Authentic Movement practice, the mover learns to become aware of her bodily, kinaesthetic sense, to track her movements over time, and to be aware of the feelings, sensations and images that evokes. This process is part of developing an inner witness. It is more common to 'observe with a critical, comparing or judgemental mind' (Weiss, 2009, p. 7) than to just observe, and this is true whether we are observing in Authentic Movement or in research practice. The inner witness can be compared to *sakshin,* the non-judging friendly witness without expectation, that can be developed through yoga (Rosen, 2002), or the Buddhist idea of an internal observer who, 'if correctly trained, will be able to look at ourselves without judgement, with equanimity, benevolence, acceptance, curiosity, passivity and calm' (Weiss, 2009, p. 7). The soul is also translated as the seer, or witness, in Sanskrit (Iyengar, 1993). Witnessing is likened by Hartley to meditation (Hartley, 2004), and can have applications beyond the form of the moving circle, in both professional and personal relationships. It is the process of sharing through words that allows the expression into language of the experiences of the body, as both mover and witness. Developing witnessing skills allows researchers to be in the moment, and remember the moment in detail. Attention to detail allows deeper reflexivity, which is essential for Embodied Inquiry. However, as with any skill, it takes time to develop and practise it.

Chapter Summary

This chapter:

- highlighted a typology of research foci for Embodied Inquiry
- outlined the basic foundations of Embodied Inquiry
- provided an introduction to multimodality, phenomenology and hermeneutics in the context of Embodied Inquiry
- offered some initial guidance regarding the practicalities of designing for and carrying out Embodied Inquiry
- considered the benefits of Embodied Inquiry

CHAPTER 4

Data in Embodied Inquiry

Introduction

Depending on the aims, purposes and objectives of a project, researchers need to think about what they consider data in their project. Traditional qualitative data includes interview transcriptions, survey results or questionnaire data, for example, and an Embodied Inquiry may do this too. However, a project focusing on the participants' lived experiences needs to ensure participants are able to reflect on their embodied experiences and are given the tools to then communicate these often-unconscious processes. Focusing on the body as a communicator or as an interactor may require participant observations as well as self-observations. A focus on embodiment does not necessarily mean that we do not trust the wealth and breadth of established data collection methods; it means that we need to restructure the emphasis of the methods. In order to design for embodiment, a clear decision will need to be made on what data are and how those data will be recorded.

Collecting, Gathering, Generating, Making Data

Before we can consider the details of how to get the kind of data that are helpful and interesting in Embodied Inquiry, we need to explore some philosophical underpinnings about data. In qualitative research methods books, authors commonly talk about 'data collection' (e.g. Cohen et al., 2013; Bryman, 2016; Walliman,

2017; Hennink et al., 2020) when they explain how to carry out interviews, surveys, questionnaires, and the like. Some, though many fewer scholars, avoid the terminology 'data collection' and, instead, use 'data gathering' (e.g. Lichtman, 2012; Silverman, 2015). On the surface, the distinction may appear minimal and negligible, as 'to gather' and 'to collect' are synonyms in the English language and the Oxford English Dictionary uses the verb 'to gather' to define, describe and explain 'to collect', and vice versa ('collect, v.', n.d.; 'gather, v.', n.d.). Within the context of qualitative research, however, the distinction is important, as it highlights an underlying philosophical viewpoint for this particular stage of the research process.

Researchers subscribing to 'data collection' implicitly align themselves with the epistemological positions that see knowledge as absolute and concrete. 'Making data' on the other end of the scale implies that there is no absolute knowledge, truth or experience, and therefore the role of the researcher is to make sense of what the participants create in a particular circumstance, situation and context. The phrases 'gathering data' and 'generating data' are located in between the two extreme ends of collecting data and making data.

Although interest in the difference between data collection and data generation has increased in the last decade, the conceptualization of data and knowledge being relational and constructed is not new. In his 1973 publication *The Interpretation of Cultures*, Clifford Geertz highlighted that

> data are really our own constructions of other people's constructions of what they and their compatriots are up to [. . .] we are already explicating: and worse, explicating explications. (Geertz, 1973, p. 9)

The distinction and the researcher's role within the different processes are best explained in the words of Svend Brinkmann and Steinar Kvale's (2015) metaphor of the 'data miner' and the 'data traveller'. The researcher as data miner considers the participants' knowledge and experience as a nugget of valuable metal buried in the soil. The 'data collection' process therefore is to unearth this nugget and dig away at the unnecessary and irrelevant elements to achieve the absolute, authentic truth. The data traveller researchers see themselves on a journey alongside the participants, where jointly they will explore experiences. Data in this context are then the conversations and the meaning-making processes between researchers and participants. This journey to new meanings is then described as a process of 'data generation'. The differentiation between data collection and data generation, between data miner and data traveller, therefore lies in how the researchers see themselves and their roles in being part of the data process. The terminology 'making data' refers to the understanding that the researcher is engaged in the data process, that the researcher cannot extract data from participants, but is intrinsically linked to and involved in the construction of data and knowledge (Ellingson and Sotirin, 2019, 2020).

Whilst what counts as knowledge can vary between as well as within disciplines (Brew and Lucas, 2009), we need to consider what embodied experiences bring to other forms of knowledge (Goellner and Murphy, 1995). At this point we would like to refer back to the theoretical foundations of Embodied Inquiry laid out in Chapter 3, building on the foundational principles of phenomenology, hermeneutics and multimodality. We also draw on features of interview knowledge, which Brinkmann and Kvale (2015) have characterized as produced, relational, conversational, contextual, linguistic, narrative and pragmatic. Embodied Inquiry then sees knowledge as produced, relational, contextual and multimodal.

Knowledge as Produced and Relational

Embodied Inquiry is not naturally occurring, but an event that is staged by a researcher for a specific purpose with a particular aim in mind. The conversations, interviews and any other data engagement are therefore social constructions with the end result of knowledge having been created or produced. Within this production process there are interactions between the participants and researchers or amongst participants in focus groups, for example. Therefore, the knowledge produced in these particular circumstances and contexts is the outcome of these interrelated connections and interactions. Due to the body in Embodied Inquiry taking a more central role, the researchers' and participants' experiences of their bodies are produced and relational to an extent that they would not be without the focus on the body.

Knowledge as Contextual

Life experiences, human understanding and communication shape and are shaped by the contexts in which they occur. With every repetition of an experience, there are some details that have changed. These changes may be due to a difference in audience or conversation partner, or they are due to our own altered understanding and life experiences as time has progressed. In any case, as humans are not static and life is not static, knowledge is not static, either. As a consequence, an interview organized with exactly the same interview questions and between exactly the same researchers and participants will lead to different responses and outcomes, simply because of the contextual shift of that interview having occurred at a different stage in the participants' life. Data in Embodied Inquiry are therefore not seen as absolute, but as produced and relational in a very specific context under particular circumstances.

Knowledge as Multimodal

As human communication is multimodal, knowledge also is multimodal, with the result that the different forms of communication, or modes, cannot be separated from one another. Knowledge may well be constituted through the verbal interaction, but even within interview studies, gestures, facial expressions or other nonverbal communication features will play a role. Embodied Inquiry therefore asks for and relies on a multimodal data set or a range of data sets in addition to interview transcriptions rather than merely accepting one modality, with participants being offered a wide variety of modes of communication to draw on for their purposes.

Generating and Making Data in Embodied Inquiry

The fact that Embodied Inquiry sees knowledge as produced, relational, contextual and multimodal has a significant bearing on the methods used during the research process. In a sensory ethnographic project that sought to understand how individuals decide which clothes are considered dirty and in need of washing (Pink, 2015), it became evident that this decision is truly embodied in that individuals use their sense of smell. In such a situation, the data collection needs to include the observation of research participants. Ideally, the researcher would record the entire observation of the participants picking up the washing basket and deciding between dirty and clean clothes. A video recording of such an observation would later allow the researcher perhaps in collaboration with a participant to identify the embodied practices involved in the process of sorting washing. Similarly, in projects that employ elements of visual communication such as photography (Guell and Ogilvie, 2015; Orr and Phoenix, 2015), metaphorical representations (Nind and Vinha, 2016; King, 2013) or models and other visual materials (Mason and Davies, 2009; Brown and Collins, 2018), the actual photographs or objects are also data in themselves.

In practice, it may not be possible for the researcher to be physically present in the very moment of the relevant action or interaction, so researchers rely on their own self-observations alongside participants' self-observations. Self-observations are not without practical concerns (Rodriguez et al., 2002; Foster et al., 1999). The parameters of what is observed and how need to be clarified. Such instructions need to be formulated clearly and succinctly, and yet in a way that they are not leading and are free from any initial assumptions or biases. Next, self-observation relies on a level of personal awareness and mindfulness that individuals may not be commonly used to. We also need to remind ourselves that we may not always be honest with ourselves, and that therefore self-observations require an openness to being truthful that may be uncomfortable, which is where the practices outlined in Chapter 2 designed to increase self-awareness may prove a useful foundation. In addition to these complexities, self-observations require the individuals, researchers and participants, to recall and report as accurately as possible what has been observed at this stage without creating interpretations or making value judgements. Data in this context are the collation of self-reported information. In other projects, this self-reported information is part of a visual diary (McDonald et al., 2017; Salmenius-Suominen et al., 2016) or photo-elicitation for interviews (Dockett et al., 2017; Bates et al., 2017).

To return to Brinkmann and Kvale's (2015) metaphor, within Embodied Inquiry the researcher is a data traveller on a journey alongside and with participants to explore and make sense of bodily, embodied, lived experiences. Therefore, what would traditionally be 'data collection' is interpreted as an organic, dynamic, fluid process of generating and making data to allow for space to practise and actively engage in the hermeneutic spiral.

Creative Methods and Arts-Based Approaches in Research

On the premise that human understanding is embodied, language is complex and communication is multimodal, Embodied Inquiry seeks to explore and understand bodily and embodied experiences. As a consequence, data generation needs to account for all of these features and elements of the research. Naturally, data generation processes include more traditional elements and conventional research methods, such as interviews, questionnaires and surveys, but they also incorporate what are often termed as 'creative' or 'arts-based' methods.

Creative and arts-based research, although linked and interrelated, are not strictly the same, and a helpful process to think about the forms of data generation available is to explore the creative and arts-based methods in a little more detail. 'Creative' refers to the connotation of 'to create' or 'to make', but also to the concept of 'creativity', which is often associated with originality, effectiveness and the ability to solve problems (Runco and Jaeger, 2012; Preiser, 2006). Due to the fact that research is unpredictable and requires the ability to solve problems and make analytical decisions, research in itself is a creative process (Kara, 2015). Creative researchers and researchers employing creative methods seek to overcome conventional, disciplinary boundaries such as the distinctions between mind and body or quantitative and qualitative research or arts and sciences (Kara, 2015). Instead, researchers actively employ creative methods to challenge and transcend such categories. In some instances, creativity and art are presented as synonymous (Hesmondhalgh and Baker, 2013; Mewburn, 2012). And whilst there certainly is a connection between the two, creative and arts-based methods are different. Some scholars divide creative research methods into subcategories, such as arts-based, narrative-based and redefined (Rapport, 2004), the last meaning using existing and conventional methods to rearrange and reuse them in a different, new way. For others, 'creative methods' or 'inventive methods' (Lury and Wakeford, 2012) are much broader terms encompassing arts-based research, but also including research using technology, mixed-methods research and transformative research frameworks, whereby the categories are again fluid and creative methods can fall into more than one of the four areas (Kara, 2015).

Like many frameworks and paradigms arts-based research has also evolved over time and so cannot be neatly packaged into one category. Depending on the focus of the enquiry, the aim of the research and the positionality of the artist-practitioner-researcher, arts-based research may be described as 'arts-inquiring pedagogy, arts-based inquiry, arts-informed inquiry, arts-informing inquiry, arts-engaging inquiry, and arts-related evaluation' (Savin-Baden and Wimpenny, 2014, p. 5). In all of these forms of arts-based enquiries, the arts are used to 'raise significant questions and engender conversations; to capture meanings; to diversify the pantry of methods that researchers can use to address the problems they care about; and to contribute to human understanding' (Barone and Eisner, 2012, p. 164–172). Employing arts-based research helps

> to provide new insights and learning; to describe, explore, discover, problem-solve; ... to forge micro-macro connections; ... to engage holistically; ... to be evocative and provocative; ... to raise awareness and empathy; ... to unsettle stereotypes, challenge dominant ideologies, and include marginalized voices and perspectives; ... and to open up avenues for public scholarship, usefulness and social justice. (Leavy, 2015, p. 21–27)

Bearing in mind these particular functions of creative and arts-based methods, it is not surprising then, that researchers engaging in Embodied Inquiry also draw on and employ creative and arts-based approaches alongside other, more conventional approaches. This is not to say that data generation in Embodied Inquiry automatically is or must be arts-based. The use and prevalence of arts-based approaches and creative methods within Embodied Inquiry are merely a testament to the strong embodied and bodily connections the arts offer.

Data Generation Methods in Embodied Inquiry

In the following, we will focus on some examples out of the incredible inventory of data generation methods within Embodied Inquiry. But before we do that, we would like to emphasize that the examples provided here are not at all exhaustive or, indeed, compulsory. Instead, the philosophical and methodological principles of Embodied Inquiry (see Chapters 1, 2 and 3) allow for eclecticism in addition to conventional data methods such as interviews, surveys, questionnaires and observations. As these are discussed in many research methods books, we focus on the lesser reported data generation methods here.

The range of individual methods in use in Embodied Inquiry is vast and includes photo-voice, video-recordings, diary methods, walking interviews, forms of poetic inquiry, creations of films, performances and ethnodrama, fictionalizations, and making and creating activities, such as collaging, model-making, map-making or mark-making. Trying to provide a complete list of all data generation methods in use in Embodied Inquiry would be an impossible undertaking, as the field is rapidly changing and because researchers engage in Embodied Inquiry without specifically referring to that.

However, we acknowledge that some guidance is useful, and so we would like to provide a brief annotated list of relevant examples in this section to offer some overview. Naturally, given our personal research interests, we are aware of a wide range of research articles using a variety of different data generation methods. If we have included a particular research publication, this is not necessarily meant to be read as an example of Embodied Inquiry, but as an example of authors having accounted for embodiment in their data collection or data generation phase that would be suitable and useful as potential methods for Embodied Inquiry. By the same token, if we have left out some outstanding examples, we would like to apologize at this stage for the oversight. In general, if you are particularly interested in non-traditional forms of data, analysis and dissemination, we recommend you regularly check the academic journals *Qualitative Inquiry, Qualitative Research, International Journal of Social Research Methodology, Journal of Contemporary Ethnography* and *International Journal of Qualitative Methods.*

Once we have listed some common methods used in Embodied Inquiry we go on to consider our own research projects in the section 'Case studies of Embodied Inquiry'.

Photographs

Photographs are often used in connection with a diary method, where participants are asked to take photographs of their experiences, or in conjunction with interviews. The photographs are commonly supplied either by the researcher or the participant and serve as a stimulus for the conversation to elicit specific kinds of information (e.g. Guell and Ogilvie, 2015; Orr and Phoenix, 2015; Bates, 2019; Watson & Leigh, 2020). In relation to Embodied Inquiry, photographs fulfil the function of being able to express and depict embodiment and experiences and representations of the body. As photographs allow individuals to experiment with what would usually remain invisible through editing, cropping or otherwise manipulating photographs, they can become particularly impactful communication tools, especially as cameras have become ubiquitous due to the development of mobile phone technology.

Arts Workshops

A participatory research approach to exploring embodiment is through arts workshops, which are often held in small groups. Depending on the aim and purpose of the workshops, the researcher may collaborate with artists in order to support the communication of the contents artistically and aesthetically (e.g. Bartlett, 2015). In the case of Tarr et al. (2018) the research team collaborated with artists who ran and delivered the workshops that the research team had organized. This workshop took on performative elements, as it included improvisation alongside data assemblage from conversation transcripts. The nature of the workshops, their aims and the delivery obviously influence how much embodiment is accounted for. Where Embodied Inquiry is concerned, the physicality of moving and improvising, or the creation of collages or other artful representations helps participants and researchers become aware of their bodies and their being-in-the-world, which in turn provides an important starting point for further exploration of embodied experiences.

Mapping and Body-Mapping

The joint creation and interpretation of maps or body-maps between participants and researchers, in particular, is commonly used in research relating to health issues and environmental concerns. In these cases, the aim for the researcher is to make visible and explicit what would otherwise remain unseen, such as locations of pain in your body or trajectories and relevance of locations (e.g. De Jager et al., 2016; Thomas and Tarr, 2009). Mapping and body-mapping therefore offer quite a different insight into experiences than photographs and arts workshops do, for example, although they all offer opportunities to make explicit what is often overlooked and engage the emotions of participants, researchers and any other audiences.

Ethnodrama or Performance

Ethnodramas and performances are often associated with performance ethnography that seeks to bring to life the research process or the outcome of a research process through a performance. There are other uses of drama with Embodied Inquiry (see for example Harvey et al., 2019; Bradley, 2020). Participants are involved in the process of scripting the play as well as in the production and post-production of the performance. Depending on the focus of the research, the performances may be very physical and intense, thereby conveying particularly well the embodied aspects of experiences (e.g. Denzin, 2003; Saldaña, 1999; Schipper et al., 2010). In the context of Embodied Inquiry, ethnodramas and performances lend themselves particularly well to engaging audiences with experience of topics such as embodiment in the context of emotions or identity formation.

Sandboxing

The method of sandboxing refers to providing a tray of sand with some figures for participants to create a narrative or recreate an experience in the sand. The advantage of the sandbox is that participants can create a 3D model or scene and physically engage with the materials in front of them. The physical manipulation of dolls and the use of representations is commonly seen in therapy settings, especially with young children, but in the case of research allows to account for embodiment in ways that traditional methods would not (e.g. Mannay and Staples, 2019; Mannay et al., 2017).

Walking Interviews

Walking interviews make research processes more egalitarian, explore participants' experiences of spaces, places and mobility and participants' performativity within space and time (e.g. Jones et al., 2008; Clark and Emmel, 2010; Evans and Jones, 2011; Warren, 2017; Harris, 2016, Butler and Derrett, 2014). Effectively, walking interviews are interviews, but with the additional benefit that they account for physical movements and allow for the researcher to be engaged with the participants through walking alongside them, thereby being able to step into the participants' shoes and developing an empathetic, embodied understanding of participants' experiences.

Fictionalization, Scenarios and Short Story Completion

Although perhaps anchored less strongly in embodiment, fictionalized accounts and the creation of short stories have become more commonly used within the scope of qualitative research. Most commonly, the researchers will provide a stimulus for a short story, present some possible scenarios or even offer a beginning of a fictionalized account. The participants are then required to respond to these stimuli by writing. Although the story completion method has gained traction in recent years (Clarke et al., 2017) despite the potential difficulties and challenges (Braun et al., 2019), the method itself is not new (e.g. Kitzinger and Powell, 1995; Whitty, 2005). Data within studies using these approaches are commonly the written, solicited narratives alongside interviews that validate or substantiate the narratives.

Case Studies of Embodied Inquiry

Using Drawings and Movement to Explore Embodied Practices

In 2016 Jennifer was funded by the Society for Research into Higher Education to explore how academics reconciled an embodied practice with their academic practice and identity, and whether it contributed to their well-being. Academic identity and the way in which we as academics construct our working and out-of-work lives has an impact on our career, health and well-being (Darabi et al., 2015; Freedman and Stoddard Holmes, 2003; Malcolm and Zukas, 2009), and yet our understandings of our own complex identities are not always easy to put into words. Academia has been described as an unpleasant place (Bloch, 2012) primarily because emotional and embodied feelings are repressed. This study set out to explore the tensions between embodied feelings and academic identities.

Jennifer wanted this project to use discipline-crossing, creative, qualitative methodological approaches (Xenitidou and Gilbert, 2012) and draw on embodied practices within its methodology. Together with thirteen participants, Jennifer gathered a variety of data to explore the research questions through dialogue, movement, mark-making, drawing and the use of film or photographic images. Authentic Movement was used with two of the participants who had experience with the practice. Jennifer took a reflexive and participatory ethnographic role (Pink, 2009) throughout, in which her voice was heard alongside that of the other participants. This allowed the co-construction of meaning and ensured that all participant voices were heard to make sense of the data, building up a mosaic of evidence that included visual and textual data.

In relation to the typology of Embodied Inquiry from Chapter 3, Jennifer's work falls into 'the lived experience', 'the researcher's body in the field' and 'the body as communicator' categories. Jennifer set out intentionally to explore the lived experiences of both herself and her participants, with an emphasis on the emotional, hard to say, and unspoken emotions and feelings around complex concepts such as 'well-being', 'identity' and 'academia'. Jennifer used her embodied experiences as a source of data and a point of reference throughout the analytic and dissemination process. For example, even in her writing she explicitly refers to her lived body, and how it sits within the world around her (Leigh, 2019c). Jennifer also used both her and her participants' bodies as communicators. In addition to artefacts created by, with, and in response to the participants (see Figure 4.1), she used film to record the sessions. All this took place in studio spaces away from the academic office associated with work. Each participant shared their embodied practice with her, whether it was martial arts, contact improvisation, or Authentic Movement as already described. These practices can be seen in the video essay from the study that was edited by Catriona Blackburn (Leigh and Blackburn, 2017).

When it came to analysis, Jennifer was inspired by Maggie MacLure's approach to data analysis (MacLure, 2003) in which she explicitly states that as researchers we are drawn to those themes and moments that resonate with us, that excite us. As such, we do not have to feel that we have to be 'fair' or 'do justice' to all the data equally, and, instead, should feel free to follow the stories that we are inspired to tell. Jennifer took an authoethnographic stance, as she was very aware that her own understanding and positionality were very much a part of the stories she would see and tell in the data. Participants were invited to be part of a participatory approach to analysis, which contributed to the self-formation of ideas through

FIGURE 4.1 *Graphite spiral.*

authentic dialogue (Gadamer, 2004). As a methodology, Embodied Inquiry evoked honesty and openness with strangers, and created a fertile ground for expression of experience, feeling and constructions of identity. However, it challenged traditional ideas of what counts as rigorous methodology and practice within higher education.

Identity Boxes to Elicit Embodied Experiences

Nicole's research sought to explore the lived experience of academic identity under the influence of fibromyalgia. Fibromyalgia is a contested condition that is characterized by widespread, persistent pain, chronic fatigue, cognitive dysfunctions, sleep disturbances and psychological disorders (White and Harth, 2001; Wolfe et al., 2010). If sensations of pain are difficult to describe under ordinary circumstances (Scarry, 1985; Sontag, 2003), then the complexity of the fibromyalgia experience is practically impossible to verbalize and explain. This is because the symptoms themselves are evasive and elusive, but additionally, a typical feature of fibromyalgia is its variability, with symptoms waxing and waning and moving and shifting over the course of days and even within hours. As the condition is invisible and contested but disabling and debilitating, individuals with fibromyalgia often struggle to communicate their experiences even to family and friends, and so draw on similes, metaphors, memes or other forms of representations to highlight what it feels like to have fibromyalgia. In contrast to most other fibromyalgia research, Nicole was particularly interested in gaining a holistic insight into the experience of fibromyalgia rather than trying to focus on individual aspects of the condition.

Having decided early on in the research process that she would use Embodied Inquiry, Nicole deliberately built on the fact that individuals with fibromyalgia often used metaphors to represent and explain their experiences. Nicole thought that if the fibromyalgia community quite naturally used metaphors, then it would only be logical to expand on the use of metaphors and representations in order to explore the physicality of fibromyalgia. Nicole used a project that drew on memory boxes that are used in cancer and dementia care (Macmillan, 2014; Nolan et al., 2001; Hagens et al., 2003) alongside the artistic work of Joseph Cornell, whose shadowboxes were installations of everyday objects to represent deeper meanings (Waldman, 2002; Sommers and Drake, 2006). Regarding the process and practicality of carrying out the identity box project (Brown, 2017, 2018a, 2018b, 2019a, 2019b), Nicole looked to the challenges and processes typical of solicited diary methods (Bartlett and Milligan, 2015).

In practice, Nicole formulated a question and asked participants to find an object or several items to represent the answer to the question and to place those objects into a box. The participants were told to send a photograph with a brief statement of what the objects were and what they stood for before the next question was released. In total, there were five questions: 'Who are you?', 'What affects you?', 'How do others see you?', 'What role does fibromyalgia play?' and 'What does life with fibromyalgia feel like?'. Figure 4.2 is an example of one such box completed by Lisa (pseudonym), which highlights her strong sense of belief and faith, but also represents her role as a mother and homemaker, as she described herself as the glue that binds everyone together.

FIGURE 4.2 *Lisa's identity box.*

Once the participants had completed all five questions, Nicole undertook an initial analysis of the boxes, which helped develop the schedule for a semi-structured, conversational interview as per Brinkmann and Kvale's (2015) conception of an interaction between researcher and participant.

In relation to the typology of Embodied Inquiry, Nicole's work falls into 'the lived experience', 'the researcher's body in the field' and 'the body as communicator' categories. At an immediate level, Nicole was interested in and explored in detail how participants felt about their lives with fibromyalgia, how they managed their symptoms and what life with fibromyalgia felt like for them. In the process, Nicole emphasized her own positionality as someone who has long-standing medical conditions and as a researcher who experienced and was aware of strong bodily reactions to the participants' stories. Finally, the body as a communicator became relevant as fibromyalgia in its psychosomatic qualities played out throughout the study with participants experiencing particularly intensive periods of pain in response to stresses and strains in their everyday lives: their bodies clearly communicated.

When the approach was explained to them, participants were generally comfortable contributing and being part of the research because they inherently understood the principles of Embodied Inquiry, having experienced the limitations of language and the need for metaphorical expression in everyday life. Although Embodied Inquiry in itself was new to the participants, the work through objects and metaphorical representations was not experienced as alien or removed from reality. However, participants did raise concerns about the relational, produced, contextual nature of their contributions, assuming and even worrying that the knowledge shared with Nicole might not be useful or relevant.

Capturing Embodied Learning and Reflection through LEGO® Models and Authentic Movement

In 2018, Jennifer and Nicole collaborated with Phaedra Petsilas from the Rambert School of Ballet and Contemporary Dance, which is part of the Conservatoire for Dance and Drama, and Catriona Blackburn, an independent film-maker. They were awarded funding from the Conservatoire for Dance and Drama to explore how reflective practice could explicitly be taught using creative approaches to undergraduate dance students (Petsilas et al., 2019), and how film and creative research methods could be used to capture that learning process and support learning (Petsilas et al., 2019). Although reflective practice formed part of the dance curriculum at Rambert, it was not explicitly taught. Indeed, due to the traditional methods of dance pedagogy (transmission from a master and correction), and although the students perceived themselves to be reflective, because they were focused on improvement to their technique, they were not aware of different approaches to reflective practice or how they might use these to move beyond a fundamental 'what', 'so what', 'what now' approach.

The project focused on fifty-second-year undergraduate dance students. The idea was to make explicit the link between their practice (dance) and the theory behind the work, rather than teach the theory in isolation. The sessions were filmed by Catriona, and time-lapse footage of the students entering, participating in, and leaving the sessions was also captured. The sessions were spread out over two terms, with times and days varying as the Rambert timetable changed weekly. On the first day the students were each handed a new blank notebook, and given sharpie pens and invited to keep a reflective journal. They were asked to keep at least one entry a week, and told that they could use images, pictures, video or audio instead of or in addition to paper.

Authentic Movement was used to frame the theory with the idea that the students would understand and be comfortable creating movement material. They were initially invited to find a space, shut their eyes and allow their body to move from felt impulses for three minutes (see Figure 4.3). They were then given three minutes in which they were asked to track, in detail, the movements they had made. In small groups they then talked about their experiences, including whether the minutes felt longer when they were moving or when they were writing. The next short movement section asked them to pay attention to the feelings they had as they moved, and then to write and to share them in the same way. The third movement section asked them about images they perceived or imagined. In this way the students were introduced to ideas around the different modalities of information or ways that we can express and communicate and feel our embodied experiences.

FIGURE 4.3 *Exploring unconscious impulses.*

In subsequent weeks the students used LEGO® to model an answer to the question 'what is dance?' and objects to answer 'who are you as a dancer?'. They were introduced to an adapted version of Brookfield's model of Four Lenses (Brookfield, 1995), Kolb's reflective cycle (Kolb, 1984) and given the opportunity to take hold of the filming themselves (Postma and Crawford, 2006). After the sessions the students were interviewed in focus groups.

In relation to the typology of Embodied Inquiry, the work at Rambert falls into 'the lived experience', 'the body as communicator', and 'the body in interaction'. The lived experience was probably the least developed foci of the three, although the research did explore the emotions and opinions of the young dancers and therefore related to the lived experience of what it means to be a dancer. However, through our focus on developing reflective practice amongst the young dancers, we placed emphasis on the body as communicator of experiences and emotions. In our attempt to explore reflective practices, we used research methods that focused on movement, dance and choreography and specifically highlighted the role of the body in interacting with others.

Whilst Nicole, Jennifer, Phaedra and Catriona were present in the sessions, their bodies as researchers in the field were not central to this study. Because of constraints around numbers, acoustics and space, the students largely worked in groups. Their interactions with each other within the space were fundamental to their experiences and learning. The students were using their deep, technical embodied knowledge of their bodies in new ways to communicate to themselves and to each other, and to convey their lived experiences as dancers.

The project was particularly interesting as it sought to shed light on an attribute that Rambert wished their dancers to show, and yet had not, up to that point, taught explicitly. The intention behind using Authentic Movement was to put forward a practical dance and movement-based model of reflective practice, and to use that as a point of reference for the theoretical models which were thought to be potentially more challenging for this group. However, the focus groups showed that the students did not see the sessions as linked to their dance classes. The studio they were in (although beautiful) was one associated with theory and book learning rather than movement. The timing between dance classes meant that the students did not know whether to cool down, rest or continue to move.

Some of the most powerful moments came from the work with LEGO® and other objects. The group was split into two for this work, with half working with Nicole and LEGO®, and the other half with Jennifer and objects. Although some of the students had put more time into the task than others, even those who grabbed an object on their way to class were able to tell a story and to make it meaningful, emotional and honest. For example, one young man used a sachet of ketchup, and talked about the sell-by date on the back, which led to a discussion about the short working-life span and pressure placed on dancers. At Rambert students can start an undergraduate degree at the age of sixteen, graduating at nineteen to maximize their professional life. Phaedra heard a Japanese student explain her choice of object (her phone) and use more words to interact and communicate with her cohort than ever before. The LEGO® models that were built within the session looked radically different from one another, but they also explored elements of age and communication. The real constant in the narratives of meanings, however, related to the role and interrelation of technique and expression within dance. This was particularly well exemplified in one student's model that looked like a tower turned upside down. In her explanation the student emphasized that there are only very few ways to getting the techniques absolutely right, but that this foundation then opens up expression and expressive performances in powerful ways.

Chapter Summary

This chapter:

- presented the philosophical differences between data collection and data generation

- outlined that Embodied Inquiry views knowledge as produced, relational, contextual and multimodal

- discussed the relevance of creative and arts-based methods in research

- provided an overview of a variety of methods used in Embodied Inquiry (photographs, arts-workshops, mapping and body-mapping, ethnodrama or performance, sandboxing, walking interviews, fictionalization)

- offered a more detailed presentation of three case examples for Embodied Inquiry (drawings and authentic movement, identity boxes, LEGO® models)

CHAPTER 5

Analysis in Embodied Inquiry

Introduction

Although increased interest in the researcher's role within research has led to some awareness and inclusion of embodiment within data collection, gathering and creation, the body is still largely absent from data analysis. As we explained in Chapter 2, however, researchers are embodied and therefore embodiment necessarily plays a role within analysis, even if this role is neglected, unacknowledged or ignored. To illustrate this point, we commence this chapter by drawing attention to how researchers deal with interview data in conventional qualitative research projects, before presenting a general introduction to principles of analysis. These principles provide the basis for a more detailed discussion on what embodiment can bring to analysis and what therefore analysis in Embodied Inquiry may look like. We conclude this chapter with a discussion on how to ensure good quality in Embodied Inquiry.

The Researcher's Body in Analysis

The first step within the analytical process usually is the phase of transcribing and familiarizing oneself with interview data. What is often forgotten is that transcription is an embodied process of actively listening to and of noting what is being said, and of making notes of or transcribing verbatim the conversation. For some, the transcription process may be computer-assisted, via speech-to-text software or transcription support, so that particular elements do not need to be typed out word by word, although, mostly, errors will still need to be corrected. For other researchers, transcribing and data familiarization are even more embodied by taking notes with pen on paper and using markers for highlighting (James, 2013). Similarly, data analysis requires researchers to engage with computer keyboards or pens and papers, and in the event of cutting and pasting, potentially the use of scissors and glue. In all of these situations the researcher's body plays a crucial role, even though the researcher may not be consciously or reflexively aware of the body that did the listening, processing and note-taking.

Although transcriptions tend to be verbatim, there have been calls within qualitative research for allowing researchers to make choices regarding which kinds of information they would like to extract from interviews (Greenhalgh, 2020; Rutakumwa et al., 2019) and therefore reduce any unnecessary transcription because of the huge

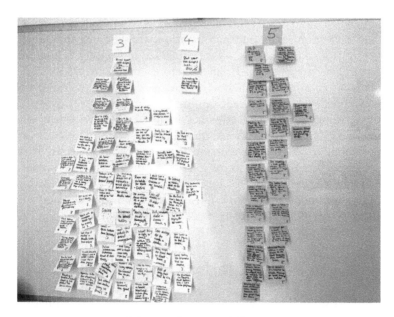

FIGURE 5.1 *Image of data analysis, initial filtering using Post-its. Ben Watson 2019©.*

burden on individuals. Another aspect to be considered in relation to embodiment is that researchers are not machines and will tire out during the process of transcribing, and thus their bodies will react differently when they try to continue listening to the transcription. By the same token, other external factors may have an impact on the researcher's body during the process of transcribing. And yet, the role of the researcher's body remains hidden and/or invisible.

Designing for embodiment in analysis means to attend to at least some of these concerns within the typology of the Embodied Inquiry laid out in Chapter 3. Attending to the researcher's experience during analysis would fit well within the scope of the researcher's body in the field. However, there are opportunities to expand on embodiment in analysis when the body in interaction is considered, as, for example, Rachelle Chadwick (2017) does in her research relating to women's experiences and narratives of childbirth. Chadwick is unsatisfied with how the typical choices made during transcribing do not provide enough insight into the embodied experience of childbirth or the embodied retelling and narrative of that experience. Instead of therefore adhering to traditional transcription conventions, Chadwick consciously chose to seek out ways to incorporate corporeality, embodiment, the body and flesh. As part of her work, she decided to create poetic representations that would highlight 'the performative qualities of birth-storytelling' (p. 63), thereby actively writing the physical interactions and expressions into the transcripts and the research.

Principles of Analysis

Before we can consider analysis in Embodied Inquiry and what analysis in Embodied Inquiry may look like, we need to reflect on what analysis is, more generally, in qualitative research. A quick search on Google Scholar, using the search term 'qualitative analysis' leads to 4.5 million entries, of which 1.7 million relate to publications from 2010 to 2020. Analysis in qualitative research is a booming business, with many different forms and typologies at the researcher's disposal. As we have highlighted throughout the book, any form of analysis is ultimately a process of choices a researcher makes. In more recent handbooks relating to qualitative research, this role of the researcher is being discussed more openly, with increasing emphasis being placed upon elements of positionality and reflexivity within research (e.g. Darawsheh and Stanley, 2014; Haynes, 2012; Pezalla et al., 2012; Alverson and Skoldberg, 2000; Barrtett et al., 2020; Langer, 2016; Walker et al., 2013). However, there is still often a gap between what researchers do and what they describe or report on what they do, with many journal articles not explicitly highlighting the role of the researcher in identifying themes or categories, for example.

There is a growing acknowledgement that the researcher takes an active role in the research process and that themes do not 'emerge', but are consciously produced, constructed and created following and relating to a researcher's personal interest (James, 2013; MacLure, 2011; Morgan, 2018; Braun and Clarke, 2006, 2019; Chiseri-Strater, 1996; Chadwick, 2017). With this in mind, analysis is then a process of reading, reflecting, interpreting, repositioning, selecting and discarding. The researcher reads the data, reflects on what they have read to come up with an initial interpretation. This interpretation stage may be linked to more reading, for example, of literature and publication to embed the interpretations in wider issues being debated. Subsequently, the researcher will reposition themselves, their data, their interpretations within this field of wider knowledge to come to a conclusion regarding which themes or topics are relevant to be selected and which are not and need to be discarded. Analytical frameworks, such as narrative analysis, content analysis, discourse analysis and thematic analysis, provide guidance, or even step-by-step instructions for carrying out the process in detail. The general principle, however, still applies: that the researcher makes choices. This is the premise that provides the basis for analysis in Embodied Inquiry.

Analysis in Embodied Inquiry

As has been outlined in previous chapters, Embodied Inquiry is a particular way of carrying out research, and this also has a bearing on how analysis is carried out. The main premise of analysis in Embodied Inquiry relates to the fact that the researcher plays an active role in making sense of data and what the data represent and show. At the same time, any analytical process in Embodied Inquiry for obvious reasons needs to account for embodiment in some form or other. Here we would like to present some examples of how embodiment can be accounted for in Embodied Inquiry analysis. We propose that there are two main ways to approach Embodied Inquiry analysis. As we will show, the first approach is in relation to the research topics and foci, which we term the 'interpretative approach to analysis'. The second approach to Embodied Inquiry analysis is through physical engagement with data that we call the 'embodied approach to analysis'.

Interpretative Approach to Analysis

As laid out in Chapter 3, Embodied Inquiry is based upon the hermeneutical tradition of iterative, interpretative analysis that allows researchers to spiral ever-deeper into their subject matter. In the context of the research foci of 'the lived experience', 'the researcher's body in the field', 'the body as a communicator' and 'the body in interaction', analysis takes on different qualities and happens at various layers. Irrespective of the research foci, Embodied Inquiry allows for a range of analytical approaches. For example, a research project into lived experiences may use interview transcripts, which can be analysed in commonly used forms and formats using computer-assisted software packages for coding and identifying relevant categories. Whether these categories are then interpreted and categorized as plots (narrative analysis) or themes (thematic analysis) is entirely the researcher's choice. To continue with this example, the key element that differentiates narrative analysis or thematic analysis from the interpretative analysis in Embodied Inquiry is that the researcher adds another layer of information and analysis through the exploration of embodied experiences – the participants' as well as the researcher's.

Although our predominant focus has been qualitative research, this aspect of interpretative analysis in Embodied Inquiry is not limited to qualitative research. Indeed, adding this extra layer of analysis may be an element to be included in quantitative projects, as all researchers will have embodied reactions to their investigations and data. At this stage, let us consider a laboratory situation, where the medical researcher meticulously watching the development in petri dishes experiences a setback, realizing that the experiments would need to be repeated in different ways because the results to date are inconclusive. It is inconceivable that such a setback would not cause some embodied reaction, such as an increased heart rate, feeling a punch to the stomach, feeling nauseated or dizzy. In Embodied Inquiry, this is important information that requires consideration and analysis.

To simplify, Embodied Inquiry offers streams or layers of analysis that work alongside and in addition to the initial interpretation of the data. Interpretative analysis in Embodied Inquiry therefore allows researchers to access more streams or layers of analysis. This is done through the researcher's engagement with their own embodiment and bodily experiences during the processes of reading, coding and interpreting. In this sense, analysis in Embodied Inquiry specifically looks at how the researcher's own embodiment and bodily experiences impact their understanding of the subject matter being considered. For example, Carolyn Ellis writes about her layered approach when writing about her experiences as her mother was terminally ill and died (Bochner and Ellis, 2016). Her initial writings were overset by conversations with her mother, and reflections of those conversations on her own and with others. She used her memory and reflections to see how the writing and paying attention to her embodied experiences in the moment changed her relationship with her mother whilst she was still alive, and the memories that she has of those times.

This approach would work for any data set. Embodied Inquiry could return to the data, after having coded them according to their preferred analytical framework. The researcher could then add in their interpretations of their own experiences, reflections from conversations they had had about the data and their conclusions with collaborators, participants or colleagues, to form a layer on top of the original analysis. As per the hermeneutic spiral, the researcher thus moves backwards and forwards between the specific individual experiences of participants and of their own selves, to the wider, more general whole of the research. Each of these layers would therefore deepen understanding in the produced, relational, contextual manner described in Chapter 4.

Embodied Approach to Analysis

If the first approach to analysis in Embodied Inquiry relies on the hermeneutic tradition of iterative interpretation, this second approach to analysis in Embodied Inquiry is closely aligned with and linked to the cornerstones of human understanding, communication and multimodality. In Chapters 3 and 4, we highlighted that language is insufficient and imprecise, that human understanding is embodied and that, as a consequence, understanding and communication are metaphorical. With these foundational principles in mind, we suggest that Embodied Inquiry should draw on multimodality to explain forms of communication and expression. This, in turn, has a bearing on how analysis in Embodied Inquiry can be undertaken. If human understanding is metaphorical and communication multimodal, then analysis ought to be exactly that, too. This is the starting point for the embodied approach to analysis.

In Chapter 3, we showed briefly that the process of analysis is in itself an embodied activity, in that it requires typing or writing, engagement with keyboards and computer software and the like. However, the role of the researcher and the researcher's body can be made to play a more important role within the analytical process if the researcher consciously chooses to physically engage with data. We have already presented the example of Rachelle Chadwick's work in relation to transcriptions. However, researchers do not need to engage with transcripts in this way (Chadwick, 2017). Instead, there are other ways to become immersed in data in a material, physical, embodied and bodily way. In the following section, we present five examples of embodied approaches to analysis in Embodied Inquiry. The examples listed here are not definitive, but are meant to provide food for thought. Other examples might include performances such as ethnodrama, film, or fiction and the like. Despite their differences in form and format, all examples have in common the researcher's preoccupation with data, which may refer to physical movements, material works or bodily engagement, such as emotional involvement.

Embodied Analysis in Embodied Inquiry

Installation

Here we draw on Nicole's research relating to fibromyalgia to demonstrate how an installation may offer a level of embodied analysis that interpretative approaches cannot. In the conversational interviews following the completed identity box projects, Nicole specifically pursued the topic of how individuals manage their life with fibromyalgia through active engagement of and with their bodies. Nicole therefore actively sought indications of where individuals expressed ways of managing symptoms, which included elements such as 'distracting from your pain', 'using heat', 'using ice packs' or 'using relevant medication'. At the same time, participants talked about the necessity of being connected to others so that they would not feel lonely or isolated during particularly difficult times. From this information, Nicole then organized and collected a number of objects that would represent these specific strategies and coping mechanisms, and brought them together in an installation, which she called 'Peace Treaty' (see Brown, 2019a, 2019b; see Figure 5.2).

'Peace Treaty' was exhibited in an art gallery in January 2018, where it spoke to the themes of domesticity and the experiences of chronically ill persons. Each object included in the final installation was a meaningful representation of the lived experience of fibromyalgia (see Figure 5.3).

The material exploration of objects and gadgets as well as the movements involved in the physical gathering and creating of the installation enabled Nicole to make sense of her data at a level that the coding of the transcriptions did not and indeed could not. It allowed for a certain closeness and immediacy to the data that fostered empathetic, embodied knowledge rather than a solely cerebral, scholarly understanding.

Illustrated Poem

This is another example from Nicole's research into fibromyalgia and academic identity, but the approach here is somewhat different to the approach taken in the installation 'Peace Treaty'. During the earlier stages of her research, Nicole became acutely aware for the first time in her life of her physical responses to what she read, when as she was reading a specific, scholarly book, she began to feel nauseated to the point of being sick. At the time, she merely noticed and made a note of those reactions. It would have been easy to 'push through' or ignore and try to forget about such responses.

FIGURE 5.2 *'Peace Treaty'.*

Over time, however, through an increased focus on self-awareness, Nicole started tuning in to these instances where her body pushed itself into her consciousness. She used these events to recognize analytical 'hotspots' (MacLure, 2011). When she came to reading, re-reading, listening and re-listening the transcripts of the conversations between herself and her participants, she ensured she did not miss any of the visceral responses she experienced. In addition to the commonly used software-assisted coding, Nicole highlighted and extracted words and phrases that she experienced as particularly impactful. Listening to her 'gut' (MacLure, 2011; Brown, 2019a), she then used the extracted phrases to create a poetic representation of participants' experiences (see Figure 5.4).

Armchair, TV and telephone:

Many of those with fibromyalgia experience flare-ups of their symptoms, which mean they become house- or even bed-bound. In those times their lives revolve around the TV set, and the telephone to remain linked to their social network and the outside world.

Blanket, hot water bottle, ice pack:

Depending on the kind of pain, people with fibromyalgia use warmth and cold to try and manage their pain levels, in addition to the medication they are prescribed.

Medication:

Tablets prescribed for fibromyalgia include pain killers, anti-depressants, anti-convulsants, anti-inflammatories. In addition, it is highly recommended to take vitamins, especially vitamin B complex tablets to support the body's self-healing properties and promote general wellbeing.

Tea and tea lights:
Many people with fibromyalgia talk about trying to relax their bodies and minds, which they do by drinking teas, lighting candles and using aromatherapy scents. It appears that those with fibromyalgia respond particularly well to fruity, lemony and flowery scents.

Book, wool and knitting needles:
Fibromyalgia can be very disabling and patients often give up their jobs. In order to keep active and maintain a purpose in their lives, they try to engage in creative activities, like knitting and reading. However, pain levels often mean that they cannot actually do the activities, and brain fog results in processing issues so that reading is also a difficult, often impossible task.

FIGURE 5.3 *List of items in 'Peace Treaty'.*

Once this basic structure of the poem was completed, with phrases from different participants set alongside one another, Nicole felt that the poem was not truly capturing embodiment and bodily responses, and, in turn, would not have a visceral effect on readers either. She therefore decided to indicate the multitude of voices represented in the poem visually by using different fonts and sizes. Finally, Nicole added a visual representation of some of the phrases that did not quite fit into the poem, but were vital in capturing the participants' embodied experiences. These were concepts and phrases

Shattered. Broken. Numb. Empty.
Physically, and emotionally.

It's very invisible.
I am sick all the time.
But it's getting worse.
It started in one bit of my body and now other bits of my body follow.
I can be as well as possible and with a full life.
But I think of myself as a perpetual patient, as disabled.

I'm fed up with it, and I'm trying to live my life without it.
My brain is working but my body can't do it.
It isn't how I thought my life was going to be.

FIGURE 5.4 *Quotes from interview transcripts.*

around 'brokenness', but also around the comfort and familiarity participants feel because they have lived with fibromyalgia for such long periods of time, although they would much rather not have to live with it at all. Nicole chose to use a shattered mug to represent the 'brokenness', but also the attachment we all experience to special objects that we do not want to throw away, even if they can no longer fulfil their intended purpose (see Figure 5.5).

For Nicole, the process of creating the illustrated poem was helpful in making sense of the participants' experiences whilst also attending to her own embodiment during the research process. As such, this is an example of how analysis in Embodied Inquiry allows for a number of layers to be incorporated and accounted for. Similar observations and reflections have been noted in the context of I-poems (Edwards and Weller, 2012; Koelsch, 2015; Edwards, 2019) and found poems (Prendergast, 2006; Faulkner, 2016).

Fictionalization

Although perhaps anchored less strongly in embodiment, fictionalized accounts and the creation of short stories, novellas

I need duvet days

Shattered. Broken.

Numb. Empty.

Physically, and emotionally.

It's very invisible.

I am sick all the time.

I'm fed up with it, and I'm
trying to live my life without it.

But it's getting worse.

My brain is working but my body can't do it.

It started in one bit of my body and now other bits of my body follow.

I can be as well as possible and with a full life.

But I think of myself as a perpetual patient, as disabled.

It isn't how I thought my life was going to be.

January 2018

Nicole Brown

FIGURE 5.5 '*I need duvet days*', *an illustrated poem.*

or novels have become particularly popular within the scope of social sciences and are starting to enter new fields of disability studies, for example. In order to make sense of her participants' experiences, Nicole also drew on the creation of short stories for analytical purposes.

Throughout Nicole's research, participants shared difficult situations, narratives of discrimination, ableism and stories of grievance procedures and tribunal panels. In many cases, individuals were concerned that they would eventually be subjected to non-disclosure agreements (BBC April 2019a, b), and so were particularly keen to have their voices heard. The precariousness participants experienced in these times meant that they were even more acutely aware of their vulnerability, should they be identifiable. Participants also worried about the reaction from colleagues, family members and friends, as in many of the narratives the social networks around the storytellers were implicated as unsupportive, distrustful, lacking understanding and empathy. In those narratives, colleagues, family members and friends were responsible for the deterioration of working conditions and the exacerbation of symptoms. And yet, the participants wanted to share their experiences and regularly commented on the importance of not being silenced, but making their voices heard loud and clear. Nicole needed to make sense of the wealth of experiences she was entrusted with, and so instinctively she started to create characters and developed stories around them. Gradually, the characters became her companions and they spoke to her when she was driving or she dreamt of them when asleep. Some of the situations described in the stories happened, others felt like they did happen or as if they could have happened. In line with the processes of thinking with stories (Frank, 2013) and using writing as a method of inquiry (Richardson, 2000, 2003), Nicole used the story-writing process to help her better understand her data. As the author of the short story cycle, Nicole merely collected, arranged, revised, rearranged and then told a new version of what she had heard. What all characters and stories have in common is that they are thoroughly embedded in the research data. 'Calm waters' is the first story in the cycle and the character presented in this story is the one constant that connects all of the stories, who are recurrent characters in each other's lives (see Figure 5.6).

'Calm waters' presents the impact of cognitive dysfunctions, perception issues and fatigue that are associated with fibromyalgia. The goldfish in the bowl of water is a commonly used metaphor amongst people with fibromyalgia as a short-hand explanation for why individuals may find it difficult to follow conversations or streams of thoughts.

The form of Nicole's short story cycle is strongly aligned with the fictionalized writings associated with arts-based approaches. We would like to mention here three very different examples from the Social Fiction series published by Brill Sense. In her novel *October Birds*, Jessica Smartt Gullion (2014) depicts life in a fictionalized town in Texas at the time of the outbreak of an epidemic. This story is told from the point of view of several characters but highlights the weekly and monthly development in the spread of the disease. By contrast, Laurel Richardson's (2020) *Lone Twin* is an autoethnographically inspired account of personal, social, cultural and political experiences of identity. Patricia Leavy's (2020) *The*

Calm waters

All things considered, I do think of myself as a writer.

I have always written – diaries, blog posts, letters, emails, texts, scrapbooks, poetry, fictionalised accounts and short stories. I have even been part of reading and writing groups to learn more about the craft of writing; and I have read about reading and writing, and reading and writing well.

But how can I sustain that writing life if I am tired?

My body is too weak to even hold the pen, let alone move it across the page. And that is despite the pens already being of the "disability kind", pens that are meant to help old people because they are losing their fine-motor skills to grip or pens that are meant for toddlers who have yet to develop their fine-motor skills to grip.

I can perhaps overcome the challenges, perhaps with the help of a computer sprawled over my lap or a Dictaphone and other recording devices, where I can pretend to have those all-stimulating conversations with my academic self.

But even if I'm somehow able to overcome the physical barriers and to bypass my body's weaknesses, what about my brain? I'm simply too tired to hold and record the conversation.

My brain is brimming with ideas, but all I can feel is the goldfish bowl that is my head, where the goldfish-ideas just wait to be caught; and I am not able to do that because as soon as I grasp at the goldfish the entire water bowl tips to one side with water lapping up at the sidewalls of the bowl. Of course, I follow that thought, reach for it, only to miss it again because the water sways the goldfish to the opposite side of the bowl. All I do is worry. I worry that my dizziness and tipsiness are visible to others. And I worry that the waves of the water will splash over on one side of the bowl washing the good, red goldfish-ideas out of my brain altogether.

What do I do?

The answer is, I don't write.

I rest to try keep the waters calm and the goldfish in the bowl.

FIGURE 5.6 *'Calm waters'.*

Candy Floss Collection tells the story of several young adults and their acquaintances as they navigate social life and work.

Collage

Collage is an arts-based method that can be used for data collection and as part of an analytic process. In Jennifer's project exploring embodied academic identity, she used collaborative collage as a mode to talk through the themes and threads that she felt were pertinent for her and her participants, and the implications for using arts-based methods in a higher education research project. She set up a session with Nicole (who had participated in the study), and Catriona Blackburn, an anthropological film-maker who was working with Jennifer to edit and construct a video essay about the project. Jennifer used two fixed cameras to record the two-hour session and together the three talked through ideas and thoughts. This conversation was later edited into 'Thoughts on Something', which was screened at Disrupticon as a short video essay on using arts-based methods (Leigh et al., 2018). The collage, and the process of making the collage, helped Jennifer to clarify her thoughts as she wrote about and shared the findings of her project. As an image (see Figure 5.7) it acted as a point of connection to her audiences as she spoke about her participants experiences of feeling as though they were being drowned by the pressures of academia.

Collage can be less intimidating than other arts-based methods, without the imperative to be 'good' or do it well. It can be used to visually map out concepts, arguments and the scope of a research project at stages throughout a study. Qualitative Data Analysis programmes such as NVivo include visual mapping tools which they suggest using to aid the analytic process. Surrounding oneself with materials related to the research, pictures, text, craft supplies, scissors and glue is a hands-on equivalent.

Ensuring Good Quality in Embodied Inquiry

Referring back to the general principles of analysis, there are many different frameworks for how quality is ensured in research (see Brown, 2020 for a more detailed exploration, upon which this section is based). Despite the fact that qualitative research is quite different from positivist frameworks, there are often mentions of 'reliability, validity, rigour and generalisability' (e.g. Morse et al., 2002; Long and Johnson, 2000; Smith and McGannon, 2018; Amankwaa, 2016). Within specific branches of qualitative research, such as arts-based research, there is a recognition that such terms and categories are not necessarily helpful in judging quality, as they do not engage with the aims and purposes of the research. As a consequence, scholars in those fields present their own frameworks and criteria, such as applicability (Lincoln and Guba,

FIGURE 5.7 *Exploring academic identity.*

1990), credibility (Creswell and Miller, 2000), fuzzy generalization (Bassey, 2000, 2001) or characteristics like worthy topic, rich rigour, sincerity, credibility, resonance, significant contribution, ethics and meaningful coherence (Tracy, 2010), incisiveness, concision, coherence, generativity, social significance, and evocation and illumination (Barone and Eisner, 2012).

With Embodied Inquiry, the generic principles of good quality in qualitative research apply, and we should not necessarily try to evaluate Embodied Inquiry in different ways. However, given the emphasis of embodied experiences and positionality within

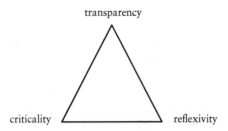

FIGURE 5.8 *Criteria for good quality research. Nicole Brown 2020©.*

Embodied Inquiry, we argue that there are basic principles underpinning analysis in Embodied Inquiry. Drawing on Brown (2019a, 2019b, p. 497, 2020) we put forward a visual representation of the three interconnected strands for ensuring and assuring good quality research – transparency, criticality and reflexivity.

These three cornerstones of good qualitative research cannot be seen in isolation from one another, but should be seen as interconnected facets of the same issue. One major criticism of qualitative and arts-based research relates to the 'anything-goes, navel-gazing' attitude that will allow individuals to engage in forms of expression that are to their liking but not necessarily scientific. In order to counteract this criticism, it is necessary to critically engage with the study and its methods, the data and their interpretation, and the choices that researchers and participants make throughout the process. Researchers need to critically view and re-view the entire research process in its individual stages in a reflective and reflexive cycle. During analysis, for example, attending to only one level of interpretation of data does not demonstrate critical engagement with the analytical process. Instead, it is necessary to look for different, potentially opposing interpretations. The critical engagement on its own, however, is not sufficient.

Researchers need to be transparent, open and honest about the choices and selections they make, the limitations and challenges they experienced, about what they do in analysis, how they do it and which thought processes go into that analytical shaping of themes and ideas. Researchers can engage critically in and be transparent about the choices they make only when they consider their personal views and the lenses through which they carry out their research. Transparency for the benefit of readers of research requires, firstly, critical transparency towards and of one's self: reflexivity.

Thinking reflexively about biases, prejudices and world views allows researchers to recognize where and how they shape data collection and analysis. Research reports and publications relating to qualitative research in the social sciences often explore elements of positionality in relation to personal biases, experiences and pre-existing knowledge brought to the research. Through detailing and exemplifying such factors, researchers seek to validate and objectivize their analyses and any potential influences on findings and outcomes, and thus to make their research 'at least quasi-objective' (Foley, 2002, p. 473). This is, however, problematic. The stages or phases of reflections and individual learning or recognition are frequently not made transparent or, indeed, critically engaged with. It is merely the researcher's final conclusion that is shared. Yet, if a researcher is truly committed to reflexivity and its 'process of self-scrutiny' (Chiseri-Strater, 1996, p. 130), then reflections about reflections or justifications must be superimposed openly and explicitly.

Chapter Summary

This chapter:

- presented general principles of analysis in qualitative analysis

- outlined two forms of analysis in Embodied Inquiry: the interpretative approach and the embodied approach

- discussed the foundational basis and some key elements in relation to the two forms of analysis in Embodied Inquiry

- provided an overview of five different examples for using an embodied approach to analysis in Embodied Inquiry (installation, illustrated poem, collage, fictionalization, scriptwriting)

- offered insights into and practical strategies for how to ensure good quality in Embodied Inquiry

CHAPTER 6

Issues and Challenges of Embodied Inquiry

Introduction

Irrespective of the research a researcher may decide to carry out and wish to undertake, there will rarely be a method which gains unconditional approval. Instead, every project requires the researcher to make trade-offs. Embodied Inquiry, with its focus on the lived, messy body and its lived messy emotions is no different. Indeed, it could be said that because of its inherent affinity for a kaleidoscope of theoretical frames, research approaches and multimodal data, an Embodied Inquiry means researchers will have even more considerations to be aware of. As we have shown, there are many opportunities for writing the body into research, but within an Embodied Inquiry it is important to be aware of and consider some implications of the approach.

In Chapter 2 we introduced the idea that Embodied Inquiry is related to psychotherapeutic interrogation, and here we consider the implications for researchers in engaging in this process, especially those who are unlikely to be trained therapists. In doing so we aim to give an overview of the challenges and issues that may arise when using a research approach that is closely aligned to therapeutic approaches. The practices outlined in Chapter 2 may be useful for researchers to develop the skills of self-awareness, honesty and reflexivity necessary for Embodied Inquiry, even if they are not trained to use them directly as research tools. We have considered what an embodied approach might bring or add to research, focusing strongly on ideas of positionality and reflexivity. Whilst it is not necessary for an embodied approach to be reflexive, reflexivity and an awareness of one's own positionality is inherently part of an Embodied Inquiry. Without it, criticisms of bias, and lack of methodological rigour and validity are fair, because an Embodied Inquiry without reflexivity and awareness of positionality is far more likely to be a projection of our own values and ideals than an open inquiry into others. Put more simply, we need to know where we are looking *from* in order to critically analyse what we are looking *at*.

Philosophical Considerations

Ethical Considerations with Embodied Inquiry

All research in this day and age needs to consider the ethical and axiological impact it may have on individuals. Recently, scholars have called for a broader understanding of ethics as a process rather than as a static task to be completed for the benefit of an ethics committee (e.g. Ramcharan and Cutcliffe, 2001; Cutcliffe and Ramcharan, 2002; Kelley et al., 2013). Influences such as data protection and increasing awareness about participatory, feminist and Indigenous approaches to research have impacted on research ethics processes (Kara, 2018). Latest ethics advice accounts for and considers in detail the kind and topic of research that is to be carried out, the participant group that is to be invited to the research, who might be excluded and the methods that are to be used, from research design through to data collection or generation and then to analysis and dissemination. There is a growing awareness that individuals who may appear privileged may actually be vulnerable in certain respects, and the definition of who is a vulnerable individual can be ambiguous.

In the context of Embodied Inquiry, these considerations are particularly important. For example, according to institutional ethics committees, it is often sufficient to ask for the informed consent of participants in relation to the contributions they make to the research. When it comes to Embodied Inquiry, and the use of photographs, personal sketches or meaningful objects, individuals may make themselves vulnerable in ways that cannot be foreseen. This is where process ethics and assent at every stage of the research are paramount (Kara, 2018, p. 103-4). It is crucial to include axiology and ethics into the heart of research design and implementation rather than just considering ontology and epistemology (Kara, 2018). Additionally, Embodied Inquiry may deal with participants' bodies and sensitive topics, perhaps exploring questions around fat-shaming, body-image or health-related topics, such as the use of stomas or the hormonal experiences of bodies (e.g. Huggins, 2016; Owens and Beistle, 2016; Westfall, 2016). In these contexts, Embodied Inquiry becomes particularly delicate requiring the researcher to find sensitivity and strike the right balance between gathering data and not forcing individuals to open themselves up to vulnerabilities that may usually remain hidden and risking harm to them.

The majority of researchers are not trained therapists. However, just like a therapist, a researcher needs to be aware of the effects on participants when they share their stories, on themselves as researchers when they hear, process and analyse this kind of work, and on audiences when findings are disseminated. Researchers need to be mindful of boundaries and limitations particularly when dealing with vulnerable groups.[1] For example, in the context of lived experiences with stoma[2] formation, participants are required to focus on their personal experiences, which in themselves are difficult to process. However, that is not all; the emphasis on the body and bodily functions means that participants may also have to approach questions of stigmatization and embarrassment, as well as the wider impact on their personal and social life, which will include thoughts around sex and sexuality (e.g. Manderson, 2005; Thorpe et al., 2016), in addition to the exploration of a failed or

---

[1] This is the subject of a forthcoming book, Leigh, J. *Boundaries of qualitative research: Between art, education, therapy and science* to be published by Bristol University Press in 2023.

[2] A stoma is a permanent or temporary opening on the abdomen that can be connected to the digestive or urinary system to allow waste to be diverted out of the body. Common reasons to create a stoma include bowel cancer, bladder cancer, inflammatory bowel disease (Crohn's Disease or Ulcerative Colitis), diverticulitis or an obstruction to the bladder or bowel.

failing body, especially when stomas are reversed and the effects are more negative than anticipated (e.g. Taylor and Morgan, 2011; Taylor and Bradshaw, 2013). In this sense, Embodied Inquiry is not considering merely the body but the participants' whole self, their identity, and their sense of being, which is why ethical considerations need to be at the forefront and centre of any Embodied Inquiry.

The moment that researchers choose to include audio-visual methods to record participant interviews, interactions or as a method in their own right (Harris, 2016), questions about anonymity are raised. Where conventional ethics processes ask to anonymize participants, it cannot be done if their faces and bodies are visible. Blanking out faces may not be appropriate or even work that well to hide someone's identity. It is possible to identify someone through even the smallest part of their body or movement. Similarly, asking participants to share objects or images that are meaningful to them means a researcher has to ensure that the individuals cannot be identified through those objects. In Chapter 5 we saw in Nicole's work with academics with fibromyalgia how she chose to tackle this by constructing an installation that was inspired by objects shared by participants, rather than the actual objects or photographs themselves.

When working creatively with and being inspired by participants, or research collaborators, there are other issues to consider. Embodied Inquiry involving one researcher is going to be different from Embodied Inquiry with two or more researchers. Two or more people can talk things through in a way that will not be the same as in the case of a lone worker. This may change the research process. Whose voices have more authority if there is a disagreement? Whose 'side' are we on as researchers (Becker, 1967), whose story are we trying to tell? In participatory research, if the participants understand that the process should give them control over what is produced and published about them, what happens if the researcher disagrees? Further ethical issues relate to ownership, or authorship of outputs. Within academia authorship can be contested enough, and disciplines vary in how they determine whether an individual should be included, and in what order (Panter, 2020). When researchers co-create with participants, or they create artefacts as part of an Embodied Inquiry, who do these creations and outputs belong to? If they are archived, exhibited, or part of a publication, who should be given authorship? At what point do artefacts become the researchers' if they create something in response to their participants?

Reflexivity in Practice

As we have emphasized throughout this book, Embodied Inquiry is a particular way of carrying out research that puts the body at the centre. For the body to be taking this central role, it is necessary that researchers become more acutely aware of their own bodies within and during the research and analytic process. In order to be reflexive, you first need to be aware of your own standpoint (Stahl, 2011). Within qualitative research, positionality and reflexivity have played an important role for a long time (e.g. Lamb and Huttlinger, 1989; Gruenberg, 1978). However, as part of Embodied Inquiry we are proposing that reflexivity and positionality take an even more focal position.

Acknowledging your prejudices, biases and personal experiences will provide you with an insight into how you engage with the embodiment of others. We would like to present one example to explain what we mean: As researchers we might have weight issues and chase diets or weight-loss schemes on personal and private levels. When we investigate body image of bulimia patients or the lived experience of pain in ballet dancers, we may find ourselves confronted by bodies that in our eyes are more accomplished and 'perfect' (i. e. meeting societal norms of thinness) than our own. What then happens in the interviews? Do we become emotional because of our own feelings of guilt, embarrassment, shame and inadequacy? Or are we comfortable discussing under-weightedness in others in view of our own over-weightedness? What influence do these experiences have on the way we continue with the questioning? We can choose to try to eradicate bias or mitigate the impact of our emotions from our research (Kara, 2018), or we can use them as an inherent part of our work, deliberately feeding them into our research process.

Being aware of one's own embodied responses and reactions provides an insight into what is relevant. Language and our use of language highlight the important role embodiment plays. Phrases like 'listening to your gut', 'butterflies in my stomach' or 'this is mouth-watering' are not coincidental. If, therefore, during the research process, a researcher feels the hairs on the back of their neck standing up, feels cold shivers running down their spine, has pain in the stomach as it cramps up, senses their heart beating faster, their breathing changing, then these are all signs that they could be 'onto' something important – they may be having a 'eureka' moment.

We are not suggesting that every minute detail needs to be recorded in an Embodied Inquiry. We are highlighting the importance of noting key experiences and critical incidents (see Flanagan, 1954 and Butterfield et al., 2005 for details on the Critical Incident Technique as a systematic research approach). It is important to emphasize here that not everything that has been noted in records or research logs will be included in the final write-up. The records and diary entries are there for the researcher to keep track of what happens, to be able to see how one's own bodily and embodied experiences impact on data and analysis.

Reflexivity is not an end point; it is not something that is done once and then ticked off from a checklist. Reflexivity is an ongoing, ever-unfurling process. Heraclitus said 'No man ever steps in the same river twice, for it's not the same river and he's not the same man' and the same holds true for researchers when considering their reflexivity and positionality. In a chapter considering an embodied, longitudinal analysis of a qualitative researcher (Leigh, 2020a), Jennifer reflected on how her research and embodied practices appeared to have run in spirals. Reflecting on an abandoned doctorate, she wrote:

> I have found myself remembering this episode in my life, when for so long it has been hidden (forgotten) as it did not feel relevant to current work. Now, like a motif introduced in an overture, it is being re-introduced, making sense of spirals, and orbits within my work. (Leigh, 2020a, p. 11 of 33)

The importance of journals, of recording what is happening now, is that it allows us to reflect back, and connect to our positionality later. The keeping of research journals, reflective logs or field notes is not a new innovation (Mills, 1959; Emerson, 1995).[3] Keeping a

---

[3]How to keep an effective research log, which notes to take or what to do with the entries in the research log is explored in detail in the forthcoming book Brown, N. (2021). *How to Make the Most of Your Research Journal*. Bristol: Policy Press.

journal is a habit that comes easier to some than others. As with all habits, we can cultivate them if we choose, through repetition and practice (Cilley, 2002).

Cultural Assumptions

Through reflexive Embodied Inquiry researchers can explore the meaning of being human and experiences of embodiment. Embodied Inquiry can be a tool to give voice to perspectives and types of knowledge that are not always acknowledged within academia. Anthropology is traditionally associated with the exploration of other cultures and perspectives. For example, Thomas Csordas developed ideas around how bodies are our vehicles for being-in-the-world, and represent us to others (Csordas, 1994). He put forward a radical role for the body: that it should be more than just a theme or an object of analysis within research, the dominance of semiotics over phenomenology, and explored the impact on the body when subjectivity and objectivity are positioned as dichotomies. Csordas used embodiment as a paradigm for anthropology to research the subject of healing, and illness (Csordas, 2002). He used an embodied framework to understand therapeutic practice, paying attention to the somatic, and being aware of cultural sensitivity around concepts of healing.

Visual anthropologist Mike Poltorak explicitly uses embodied perspectives in order to authentically capture the perspectives of another culture in his documentary film *The Healer and The Psychiatrist* (2019). The film focuses on traditional healer Emeline Lolohea, who treats people possessed by spirits, and Tongan public psychiatrist Dr Mapa Puloka. The documentary aims to contribute to the increasingly important conversation around the growing global mental health crisis.

At this point, we would like to highlight that the dominant Euro-Western systems of research favour particular forms of knowledge and the theoretical and methodological perspectives associated with them. As Helen Kara says:

> A highly valued word in Euro-Western research is 'rigour'. This usually refers to reliability, validity, and auditability. It is interesting to note that 'rigour' is a synonym for 'inflexibility'. (Kara, 2018, p. 82)

Euro-Western paradigms of research may remain concerned with validity, representativeness and reliability; however, they rarely go as far as to say that research is valid, authentic, and must accurately reflect and build upon the relationships between the ideas and participants as in embodied or non-Euro-Western centric paradigms. The analysis must be true to the voices of all the participants and reflect an understanding of the topic that is shared by researcher and participants alike (Wilson, 2008).

Embodied Inquiry can be thought of as a development of qualitative research methods that takes the critique of conventional methods such as interviews (Oakley, 1981) further. However, it can also be approached as an alternative paradigm for research that stands alongside non-Western forms of research as it privileges different forms of knowledge, and foregrounds reflexivity and self-awareness akin to Indigenous perspectives. It is important to acknowledge one's personal subjectivity in the research one is undertaking. Through the acknowledgement of one's bias, one ensures that one's perspectives are not hidden (Sherwood, 2013).

There is a lack of diversity in academia, and many barriers placed in the way of people who are 'different', for example people of colour, those from Indigenous backgrounds or those with disabilities, from progressing within its structures. Those who are successful often achieve this at great personal cost (Fryberg and Martinez, 2014). The bodies of knowledge, the *corpus* for students, often reflect this lack of diversity, and privilege of Euro-Western forms of knowledge and research, leaving some bodies, and types of bodies, absent. One way to tackle this is to decolonize reading lists, ideally by engaging students and staff together (Jivraj, 2019). Dave Thomas describes the need for this in relation to reducing the attainment gap between students of colour and white students (Thomas, 2020). Students and staff need to be allowed and encouraged to use reading material and resources that more authentically represent the variety and breadth of the world we live in, and the kinds of knowledge that we can generate and explore as researchers. Doing this will help to provide an environment that is more supportive to those currently marginalized or 'othered'. Theoretical approaches such as Critical Race Theory (as used by Thomas) and Feminism foreground reflexivity and the importance of subjective knowledge, which is inherent in Embodied Inquiry.

Of course, there are many ways besides race that bodies can be 'othered', for example by gender. Within academia women are disproportionately adversely affected by funding structures, academic culture and caring responsibilities. In order to be intersectional, as per Kimberlé Crenshaw's definition (1989), researchers then need to ensure that narratives and research do not centre the experiences of white women in order to represent the experiences of all women (Shelton et al., 2018). At the time of writing, we are in the grip of the global Covid-19 pandemic. Many countries are locked down, with schools, universities and businesses closed. Some see lockdown as an opportunity: 'If you don't come out of this Lockdown with A New Skill, More Knowledge, Better Health & Fitness, you never lacked time. You lacked discipline [*sic*]' (@MrMotilalOswal, 2020). However, the situation is already exacerbating gender inequalities (Flaherty, 2020), with women bearing the brunt of caring responsibilities. Those with young children are expected to 'home-school' them in addition to working from home.

The Covid-19 pandemic highlighted more ways bodies are othered. For example, in certain countries Black and Brown bodies are dying at a much higher rate than white bodies (Siddique et al., 2020). The 'value' attached to certain bodies (or the lack thereof) is not equal, with mandatory DNR (do not resuscitate) notices applied to people with physical disabilities, intellectual disabilities and chronic illnesses. Their bodies are literally seen as of less value to society, and not worth the cost of attempting to treat them (Butler-Warke and Hood, 2020). Embodied Inquiry is perfectly placed to investigate the intricacies and emotional aspects of lived experiences such as these.

Methodological Considerations

Using Methods of Embodied Inquiry

When it comes to the practice of Embodied Inquiry, much of what we have suggested here is the necessity of finding methods and approaches that allow the capture of several modes, or types of data. Embodied Inquiry has an emphasis on the felt, the unspoken and the hard to capture as much as it does on words that are spoken. As seen in the examples we have shared, creative and arts-based approaches to research fit well within an Embodied Inquiry. Arts-based research can be seen as an ontological shift (Jagodzinski and Wallin, 2013), or part of an arts-based research practice (Barrett and Bolt, 2010; Leavy, 2015). It can incorporate narrative (Clough, 2002; Leavy, 2016; Snowber, 2016), metaphorical representations (Lakoff and Johnson, 2003), LEGO® (Gauntlett, 2007) and film (Harris, 2016). Arts-based and creative methods are not 'new', in that they have formed part of arts practice, therapeutic work and qualitative research for some time now (Kara, 2018; Denzin, 2010). However, in some fields, such as higher education, creative approaches are still seen as innovative (Brown and Leigh, 2018).

The exact approach taken will largely depend on individuals' knowledge, expertise and, to an extent, their courage and capacity in getting participants on board with what is planned. There are some specific considerations to be taken into account for different types of creative approaches, which are briefly outlined in the following sections.

Arts Materials, Objects and LEGO®

Arts materials are a broad category that can include drawing, painting, mark-making, collage and the like. When reflecting on a study that involved young children aged four to eleven years, Jennifer wrote:

> The quality of the materials was important, as it differentiated the work from that of 'ordinary' class materials and encouraged them to participate (Coad, 2007). Drawing and mark-making were used as an 'avenue for young children to express their views and experiences' (Clark, 2005). The act of creating a drawing can be seen as a process of learning and research (Hay and Pitchford, 2016). These methods provided a way of allowing the children to reflect, to express themselves and allow their experiences and voices to be heard. (Leigh, 2020b, p. 136)

Using high-quality materials adds to the tactile, physical nature of using arts materials. A space laid out with canvases, cartridge paper, paints, oil-pastels, lino cutting and material for collage such as printed paper, newspapers, magazines, cord, trims, sequins and glitter can be used for collaborative or individual artefacts. However, it should be noted that such materials are sensory and people respond differently to them. For example, if we consider sandboxing or the use of glitter, not everyone will enjoy the touch of them. If it is appealing to experiment beyond using felt-tip pens and thin paper, it is more likely that participants will want to join in and play. Some people will still see arts materials and expect to have to draw something 'good'. As children many of us believed that art was something that you were either 'good' or 'bad' at. If participants perceive themselves to be 'bad' at art, they may be unwilling to try. Ways to combat these feelings of not being good at art include collaborative projects, with the researcher joining in and creating their own artefacts alongside the participants, making the creation of the object secondary to the conversation, using collage, as this can be less intimidating for many, and using objects. The use of objects, collages or LEGO®, as we saw in the case studies in Chapters 3 and 4, takes the aesthetics out of the equation, so people are happier, and less intimidated by the need to be good at it (Leigh, 2020b).

Objects can be items that the participants themselves bring that have special meaning for them, or ones they choose from a selection that researchers provide. These might include figurines, animals or household objects, for example. Objects could be incorporated with other arts materials, with the stories that are told about the metaphorical representation of the choice and the meaning behind the choice being of equal value to any 'scene' created with them (Mannay et al., 2017). If participants bring or share their own objects, then this can cause issues with crossing boundaries from research into therapy, as these methods can induce sharing of emotions and stories, which they would not otherwise do (Brown and Leigh, 2018).

Using LEGO®, as in the case study at Rambert in Chapter 4 and in much of Nicole's work (Brown, 2019c; Brown et al., 2018; 2019; Brown and Collins, 2018), is another way to avoid participants feeling that they are not good enough at art. If you ask someone to draw a circle, they may worry that it is not exactly round; however, if you ask them to build a circle out of LEGO®, then they know that their circle can only be blocky and imperfect. As with objects, the stories behind the models participants make can be as valuable for data as the models themselves. Some participants may find LEGO® infantilizing, others may perceive it to be too restricting. It also should be noted that LEGO® is expensive, though possible to buy second hand, it is easy to lose little pieces each time it is used, and it is heavy to carry and transport.

With all arts-based materials of this kind, it is important to be clear about time and how much is allowed for the activities. Will participants be allowed to dip in and out as part of a conversation? If it is a group activity, it is important to note that with collage in particular, some will be happy to continue for a long time, whilst others will finish very quickly.

Movement

Movement is another arena where it is likely that participants have barriers to participation depending on how it is framed. As with art, movement can be perceived to be something that they can do, or cannot do. However, our bodies are moving through space all the time (McCormack, 2013). We can consider recording the movements participants make during interviews and other data collection activities (e.g. arts-based methods as suggested earlier), using time-lapse to capture movements and rhythms over time in space (Lyon, 2019), walking interviews, and mapping spaces. Authentic Movement has been outlined as a research approach, used as a case study in Chapter 4, and has much to offer when theorizing and explaining Embodied Inquiry. It can be used for self-development or as a basis for a research approach (Bacon, 2010). However, because it is a therapeutic process and method in its own right (Adler, 2002) it is not suggested that those inexperienced in its form employ it directly as a tool for research.

Capturing Embodied Inquiry

Film and audio-visual recording are a valuable part of Embodied Inquiry. Film can be used directly as a method to capture a research process, during analysis, and to create a mode of dissemination (Harris, 2016). It is important to be aware of what filming is intended to achieve, and the eventual use to which it will be put. Reflecting on a project where filming was initially intended to be used for analysis, then was put to use to make a video essay, we wrote:

> When Jennifer filmed her playdates, she mostly used her laptop. The resulting footage was not always the best quality. The angle was fixed, and did not always show both her and the participants. The sound quality and lighting were often poor. Two sessions were lost when the integral camera failed. These technical difficulties impacted the choices that were made in the video essay. However, they did not impact on the quality of the research project, as these methods were used in addition to digital recorders, and transcriptions of the meetings. Jennifer's reflections around the difficulties of dealing with the film footage led to her bringing in an expert and producing more and different outputs from those originally envisioned. (Brown and Leigh, 2018, p. 60–61)

Cameras in phones are ubiquitous, and movies can be filmed on an iPhone (Erbland, 2018). A phone with enough battery and memory may be the best and easiest option to record a session, or to ask participants to take and share images. If a researcher wants to use film to capture processes and to analyse multimodal data, then using footage in conventional qualitative software analysis programmes may be more than adequate. However, if there is an intention to have a film or video research output (as discussed later), then the quality of the image, sound and recording are vital. In addition to choices of camera, for example, hand held camcorder, Digital Single Lens Reflex, GoPro-type portable camera and sound recording equipment, an embodied inquirer will need to consider storage, as footage takes up a lot of memory, and editing software and skills. If researchers know they would like to create a video essay or documentary, then it is worth considering engaging an academic film-maker and editor at the beginning to assist with the process.

Forming Relationships, Exposure, Validation and Other Practicalities

Within Embodied Inquiry there are additional practicalities that researchers need to be aware of. Some of these relate to the design and implementation of the study. If and when working with collaborators, it is important to be aware of disciplinary differences, and different aims, purposes and understandings. For example, an artist might want to pursue 'aesthetics' in ways that the researcher may not be interested in. There are many relationships that individuals rely on when undertaking research, and these are often 'hidden', for example, when going about the process of setting up and funding work, or explaining it to outsiders (Shakespeare et al., 1993). Embodied Inquiry is a method that some people intrinsically understand; however, it can be hard to find support from those who 'don't get' the research approach.

As explained in earlier chapters, there are elements of reflexivity, positionality and self-reflection that are fundamental to Embodied Inquiry, and these can be developed through practices such as those outlined in Chapter 2. As an embodied inquirer you also need to ensure that you consider the emotional toil of your work and implement sufficient self-care (Ellingson, 2017). If you fail to look after yourself, then it is more likely that you will burn out. Practically, self-care might include supervision including reflecting on the relationships within your research study, decompressing from your research before you transition back into everyday life and creating boundaries to keep your work separate. Researchers need to build relationships with and be aware of their participants (or subjects of research), which may entail a certain amount of self-disclosure, and they also need to consider and be aware of themselves.

As already mentioned in this chapter, when embodied, creative research approaches are used, the boundaries between research, art and therapy can become thin[4] as illustrated in Figure 6.1.

You need to be aware of your and your participants' emotions, and how you can work to regulate and maintain them:

> Within this context of deep reflections and the participants' readiness to share experiences more openly, we do need to consider the consequences of using creative and playful approaches. The creative and playful approaches certainly encourage and capture the emotional, sensory and real experiences of participants.

---

[4]This is the subject of a forthcoming book, Leigh, J. *Boundaries of qualitative research: Between art, education, therapy and science* to be published by Bristol University Press in 2023.

However, this can mean that even innocuous subject matter touches on deep and personal stories. When these are shared both the researcher and researched are left vulnerable if they are unable to contain and process those emotions. Whereas a counsellor or therapist would have specialised training, resources and support in order to have boundaries around painful or personal material that is shared (Rogers, 1967), a researcher is unlikely to have the same. This means that issues such as transference, burn-out and knowing when and how to end a relationship with a participant are beyond the scope of many researchers (Leigh, 1998). Similarly, a participant may not expect to enter into such a personal and vulnerable space within the bounds of a research project, and without a qualified and experienced person holding the boundaries of that experience to ensure that they are contained, they may be left re-traumatised. Having said that, the creative and playful engagement in non-judgmental environments and contexts is often experienced as cathartic or revelatory. (Brown and Leigh, 2018, p. 59)

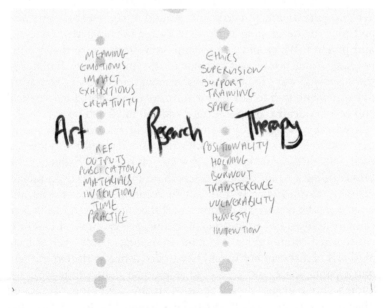

FIGURE 6.1 *The boundaries between art, research and therapy. Jennifer Leigh 2018©.*

Considering Dissemination
of Embodied Inquiry

Having considered the potential challenges and issues inherent in Embodied Inquiry, the researcher can then consider how they might 'perform' embodiment. They may use the example of poetic representation in Chapter 5 to lead into another practical concern with and around Embodied Inquiry: dissemination. Depending on where on the continuum of Embodied Inquiry a researcher finds themselves, dissemination may or may not require specific consideration.

As we have mentioned before, although the physical, material practice of doing research is not at all disembodied or unembodied, the body is regularly written out of research articles. However, embodied dissemination is quite commonly employed in some fields, such as in the creative and performative disciplines. Under the umbrella term of 'practice as research', data and findings are communicated and disseminated in performances, through artefacts or compositions (Saldaña and Omasta, 2016; Saldaña, 2015). Writing performance poetry and ethnodramas, creating artefacts and films or developing performances requires expertise, training and practice. We would like to state very clearly here that we are not suggesting researchers attempt to disseminate their findings in those specific ways by themselves, although researchers may want to experiment with some of these forms of expression, for analytical and communicative purposes (as discussed in Chapter 5).

Generally, designing for embodiment in dissemination means that researchers consider the roles their bodies and the bodies of their audiences play in making sense of research findings. This brings us back to the aims of research, as they will have an impact on what a researcher would like to communicate and why and how, once the research is completed. If the aim of the research is to raise awareness or initiate social actions, for example, a carefully constructed ethnodrama or film screening could be crucial. Similarly, if a researcher would like to do justice to the experiences participants share and create an emotional connection with the audience, a collage of photographs or an exhibition of curated objects may be needed. If researchers would like to create a film screening, they need footage, and photographs or objects to be able to create the exhibitions.

However, it is not enough merely to have some photographs or some footage; they do need to be of a high enough quality for an editor to be able to work with and on them. The real reason for considering embodiment in dissemination therefore is not so that the embodied inquirer would create and curate, but that they plan ahead, involve specialist collaborators or enlist expert consultants from the early stages. A particularly successful and exciting example for a film as a social science research output is *Rufus Stone* (Jones, 2012). The thirty-minute film depicting positioning, ageing, and gay life in rural South West England and Wales is a fictive reality based upon the narratives and incidents gathered as part of a funded research project (Jones, 2013). The film is the culmination of the collaboration between the principal investigator Kip Jones, who developed the story and characters, Director and Screen Writer Josh Appignanesi, Director of Photography Annika Summerson, Producer Cecilia Frugiuele, thirteen actors listed as cast members and a further thirty crew members who dealt with all aspects from costume design, camera, lighting and sound through to make-up and special effects (*Rufus Stone*, n.d.). An undertaking of that magnitude clearly needs meticulous planning, budgeting and scheduling. But even a smaller or shorter project cannot be a simple add-on, but will require careful thought from the outset.

As we have already mentioned, using film and audio-visual methods can be an integral part of an Embodied Inquiry. There are specific academic outlets that accept video submissions, such as the *Journal of Embodied Research* (https://jer.openlibhums.org/), and the *Journal for Video Ethnography* (http://www.videoethno .com/). Ben Spatz, a non-binary researcher within the discipline of drama, advocates audio-visual methods as the optimal method for researching and disseminating embodied experience (Spatz, forthcoming). Ben builds on their earlier work, positing the site of an Embodied Inquiry as a 'laboratory' (Spatz, 2020). Film is a powerful tool for affecting our audiences (Wilson, 2018), who respond and react to representations of the body when they see them on film, even allowing them to change their behaviour (Bowman, 2019).

When writing about the body, and embodied experiences, it is important to be aware of the difficulties. As with all academic writing, researchers need to keep in mind what they want and need to write. If researchers want to demonstrate academicity, then they may need to focus on peer-reviewed journal articles, book chapters and monographs with respected publishers. However, if including images from research is integral to dissemination, then it may not appeal to more traditional outlets. Embodied Inquiry may still be viewed as 'innovative' and risky. As an embodied inquirer, you need to think about the aspects of the study you want to focus on: the methodological process; the research findings; the implications of the research; or all of these. When you have chosen what you want to write and where you would like to publish, you then have to consider how you can write to foreground embodied experience. There are tensions and complicities between dance and writing (Lepecki, 2004), and it is easy to extrapolate this to embodiment and writing. How do you ensure that the presence of the body is on the page? You can learn how to notate and understand the qualities of the moving body (Newlove and Dalby, 2004). You can do your best to ensure that your own and/or your participants' authentic embodied experience reflected in your words (Ellingson, 2017). Again, if we look at Authentic Movement, it ritualizes the use of the present tense when writing or speaking of movement experiences in order to differentiate it from more conventional modes of communication. This is a very powerful technique, and one that any new Embodied Inquirer may use, though it takes practice to do well. This type of differentiation allows the author to separate embodied experience, remembered reflections and more academic narratives.

We must note, however, that academic research outputs are not the only forms of dissemination that can arise out of Embodied Inquiry. Fiction (Leavy, 2016), poetic inquiry (Snowber, 2016), video essays and artistic installations are all possibilities. However, depending on your home discipline, they may not be considered 'legitimate' or 'relevant' outputs of research. This may not be your primary concern, or even if it is, these outputs can still prove valuable to garner public engagement, and to engage a more traditional research-orientated audience in your work.

Chapter Summary

In this chapter we have considered:

- philosophical issues inherent within Embodied Inquiry, such as ethics, practical reflexivity and the dangers of making cultural assumptions

- methodological issues around the practicalities of using creative methods including arts-based methods, collage, LEGO®, movement as a research method and how these might be captured

- the importance of self-care, and care of others' emotions

- how we might disseminate the findings of an Embodied Inquiry.

CHAPTER 7

Embodied Inquiry Now and in the Future

Introduction

In this book we have seen how Embodied Inquiry can form part of a research study or be fundamental to any aspect of it. It can be used as a method, or to inform an arts-based approach. It can be used as a radical epistemology, influencing the very questions and ways that we approach research. In this book we have done our best not to be prescriptive about how you might go about this. Instead, we have set out to demonstrate how you might incorporate elements of Embodied Inquiry into your theoretical framing (Chapter 2), research design (Chapter 3), methods (Chapter 4) and analysis (Chapter 5), and we have presented issues and challenges that arise from this kind of work (Chapter 6). In this final chapter, we review some of the underlying principles of Embodied Inquiry, and consider how and where it might fit into wider academic research.

What Makes Something an Embodied Inquiry

In Chapters 1, 2 and 3 we highlighted that embodiment, and embodied and bodily experiences lie at the core of Embodied Inquiry and that this kind of research can be described as a continuum from little, superficial or minimal consideration of the body or embodiment through to the body and/or embodiment being integral to research (see Figure 3.1). Here, we would like to further clarify what makes a research project an Embodied Inquiry, and consider when something is *not* Embodied Inquiry. In order to do this we will return to the three basic principles of Embodied Inquiry first outlined in Chapter 1:

> The first principle sets out the 'What?' of Embodied Inquiry. Any Embodied Inquiry is part of an ongoing process of self. It asks for reflexivity, an exploration, attention to and non-judgemental awareness of self in addition to attention, exploration and non-judgemental awareness of others' experiences. Awareness of every movement and moment is a skill that can be learned and practised. It is likely to impact on life outside of the research study.
>
> The second principle answers 'Why?'. The starting point is that the body and mind are connected. By accessing the information, data and stories that bodies store, hold and tell, it is possible to reach deeper, emotional, and authentic truths about lived experience than are accessed by more conventional research techniques.
>
> The 'How?' of an Embodied Inquiry is through conscious awareness, or the intention to incorporate this way of working into research. Not each Embodied Inquiry will look the same, nor will it necessarily feel the same for the researcher or participant. However, each Embodied Inquiry will either have explicitly defined these principles or at least implicitly adhere to them.

We have highlighted throughout the book that there is no one unifying theoretical framework underlying Embodied Inquiry. There is a long history of movement forms and practices that foreground the body-mind connection and embodied experience. Any or all of these could form the basis of Embodied Inquiry. These three principles of reflexivity, conscious awareness and the interconnection of body and mind are the closest we get to a philosophical outlook within Embodied Inquiry. Merely paying attention to a body or bodies, but without reflexivity or an underlying theoretical stance that the body and mind are connected, would therefore make a study a 'body inquiry' rather than Embodied Inquiry.

For example, Laura Ellingson (2017) describes processes of 'making sense of stylized acts' and asks the researcher to 'select an identity being performed by one or more of your participants and list as many stylized acts as you can that contribute to your perception of that identity' (p. 75). Such a practice, if performed without attention to the first principle (that is, reflexivity, positionality and highlighting your own responses to those stylized acts) could easily become judgemental of others and superficial. There is a difference between judging others' embodied actions and owning your own perceptions of an event: 'I saw the sides of his mouth lift and imagined that he was smirking at me' is very different from 'he smirked'. As a researcher it is important to foreground and acknowledge your own reactions. You can only truly and authentically know your own experience, not that of others. This is not to say that in order to understand Caesar you have to be Caesar, or that all research has to be collaborative to get participants' authentication of researchers' interpretation, but more that we need to be aware of the limits of what we do.

Similarly, it is possible to imagine a scenario when there is still a disconnect between the essential *you* and the body you inhabit, that is, without attention being paid to the second principle. Some traditional sociological frames bring attention to the body whilst still objectifying it, and terming it 'the body' rather than 'my body' (Evans et al., 2004). Attributes of the body rather than embodied experience of the owned body are investigated. The body is presented as an object, with either its performativity (Butler, 1993), aesthetics, (Irvin, 2016) or appearance (Buote et al., 2011) as the focus.

Considering the third principle, is wanting a study to be Embodied Inquiry enough to make it one? From our perspective, designing a study, consciously collecting or analysing data, or disseminating research with awareness and conscious thought about Embodied Inquiry, its implications and challenges, will ensure that it is one.

These principles are necessarily not absolutes. Of course, as EI becomes more established, particular ways of working with it will emerge and in time become distinct strands or even schools, just as has been the case with numerous methodological innovations previously – grounded theory being one well-known example (Tarozzi 2020). How does a researcher know if they have sufficient awareness and conscious thought about Embodied Inquiry? In counselling, where a principle of client-centred approaches is to hold the client in unconditional positive regard (Rogers, 1967), some therapists find this hard to achieve. In order to safeguard clients, therapists must have regular supervision, where they can talk through and discuss their client load. This process is ongoing and mandatory whilst in practice. We suggest that if such supervision is not possible, then a minimum requirement for Embodied Inquiry is the ongoing process of reflexivity and attention to what is happening.

Being an Embodied Inquiry Researcher

Different theoretical conceptions and understandings of embodiment will result in different research designs, methods, analytic techniques and modes of dissemination. However, they can all incorporate elements of Embodied Inquiry. There are many reasons to use Embodied Inquiry as a main focus or part of a research study. Embodied Inquiry can engage audiences and participants (Ellingson 2017). It can be a means to process lived experiences and to make sense of them (Snowber, 2016). It can bring depth to qualitative inquiry (Denzin, 2010) by deepening the ability to listen and see what is happening (Back, 2007). Although primarily talking about children, this quote applies to work with any research participant, or person:

> Listening is a dynamic process that is not just the extraction of information from children. It involves them and adults discussing meanings, whilst avoiding giving the children cues or assistance (Irwin and Johnson, 2006). Listening means not trying to guess what the children are saying (Mauthner, 1997). It includes all the different verbal and non-verbal ways in which children communicate. This is where creative research methods can be valuable, as they allow for sharing rich experiences, without exclusively relying on the spoken or written word. (Leigh, 2020b, p. 134)

The process of listening and reflecting does not end when the research is over. In a funders' report from an Embodied Inquiry, Jennifer wrote:

> One of the interesting aspects of this study was the way in which the participants interacted with the creative research methods

and the multimodal data that was produced. As an academic it is challenging to allow data to be seen as outputs of research without a written narrative, a more conventional research output. An embodied or posthuman approach to research is inevitably messy, as it echoes the messiness of life. It invites us as researchers to challenge and question the ethics around participation and co-production of knowledge. Are we equipped to support and enable our participants to deal with the raw, honest and vulnerable emotions and feelings these approaches may generate? Are we skilled enough to hold the space for them to do this, and supported enough to seek the supervision we need to process it? The 'messy' data that this research generates again invites us to question around how we go about analysis, how honest and open and vulnerable we want to be within the research and in the telling of the stories of the research. The analytic process and frame is not clear cut and simple. It transgresses boundaries of what is research, what is therapy, what is process work, and what is art. Using creative methods can lead to questions of rigour and validity of the research. These approaches require a high degree of reflexivity and an awareness of the literature in order to frame the context, content and methodological choices. (Leigh, 2018, p. 4)

We have emphasized the value of incorporating creative methods and multimodality into Embodied Inquiry in order to reflect the messy reality of lived experience and emotions. This is not essential. Embodied Inquiry can be used to challenge traditional dissemination practices and questions of what counts as rigour and validity. If we think back to Helen Kara's association of rigour as inflexibility (Kara, 2018), then it becomes a concept that is less appealing to an embodied researcher. Bodies and minds work best when they are strong *and* flexible, and it is not a stretch to imagine that research is the same. It needs to be subtle, and reliable, so that the audience can have confidence in its findings (Payne & Payne, 2004), whilst also evoking a response and convincing them of its importance (Wilson, 2018). However, when we consider dissemination it is important to consider the implications in the context of academics needing to produce recognized research outputs in order to develop their careers.

The main characteristic of Embodied Inquiry is that it is found across many disciplines and practices, moving beyond the confines of Practice as Research (Trimingham, 2002), a methodology accepted in dance, drama, music, creative writing and the like. For example, Majorie O'Loughlin (2006) has explored educational implications, Derek McCormack (2013) brings awareness of the body into cultural geography, dance, philosophy and performance, Fransisco Varela et al. (1993) dialogue between cognitive science and meditative psychology and Ben Spatz (2015) positions embodiment as an alternative epistemology for practice and research within drama and performance studies. These few examples demonstrate the wide appeal of and for Embodied Inquiry. Indeed, there are many reports of research projects available that we would classify as Embodied Inquiry, with some notable examples being Sweta Rajan-Rankin for her work on race, bodies and embodiment (Rajan-Rankin, 2018); Jen Tarr's embodiment and mapping of pain in dancers (Tarr and Thomas, 2011); Aimee Grant's work on the embodied experience and perceptions of breastfeeding (Grant, 2016), and the embodied reactions of shock and offence to documentary analysis (Grant, 2018b); Dawn Mannay's use of sandboxing to explore the experiences of mature students and children in care (Mannay et al., 2017); Karen Morash's doctoral work arguing that the act of writing for performance needs to be embodied (Morash, 2018); and Dawn Lyon's visual ethnography and rhythmanalysis of fishmongers (Lyon and Back, 2012). Although not every one of these researchers may have called their work an Embodied Inquiry, we can see that the popularity of this research approach has increased and is continually growing.

The advantage of the wide appeal of Embodied Inquiry may at the same time represent a risk. First, because of its lack of a singular framework prescribing how to carry out data collection, analysis and dissemination, Embodied Inquiry may be seen as atheoretical and unscholarly. Nothing could be further from the truth. We highlighted the foundations of Embodied Inquiry in Chapters 1 and 2 and we summarized the three basic principles of Embodied Inquiry in this chapter. What is true, however, is that these are principles and foundations, not prescriptions and therefore Embodied Inquiry evades clear categorisations and classifications, wherein lies the second risk for an Embodied Inquiry researcher. The work Embodied Inquiry undertakes and deals with, spans and transcends conventional theoretical approaches and traditional disciplinary boundaries. Whilst this may be seen as innovative, original in some contexts, it may also be criticized as incoherent and unsubstantiated. The risk for researchers, especially for early career researchers who are in the process of still building their academic profile, is that their Embodied Inquiries will not gain the recognition they may deserve, a fact that we have also discussed in Chapter 6.

The third and, in our view, the most important risk is that which a true Embodied Inquiry brings to the researchers themselves. Engaging with one's own positionality, immersing oneself in reflexivity, developing conscious awareness and self-awareness alongside embracing the interconnection of body and mind constitute a transformative and revelatory process. We mentioned the need for self-care and for developing skills and strategies to support one's own emotions as well as the research participants' emotional well-being in Chapter 6. We are raising this point again because it is all-too-easy an element to be overlooked. Also, being reflexive and analysing one's own positionality, physical and emotional reactions in that way means to make oneself vulnerable. In her keynote talk at the fourth annual qualitative research symposium held at the University of Bath, Sara Delamont (2018) warned about that kind of vulnerability. She highlighted the relevance and importance of positionality and reflexivity, but at the same time explained how positionality statements in research articles define a researcher in a way that they may not want to be defined or known as in their careers. Delamont reminded delegates of the many warnings relating to social media posts and the potentially destructive force of badly chosen posts and photos, and likened these to the statements published in academic journals. We wholeheartedly agree. Agreeing to being wary and careful about one's representation in public and being reflexive, consciously self-aware and fostering the body-mind connection are not mutually exclusive. Embodied Inquiry does not demand the laying bare of minute or intricate details that may embarrass, shame or marginalize researchers or participants. Embodied Inquiry does demand being reflexive, consciously self-aware and fostering the body-mind connection, but how much of that process is publicized and published should and must lie in the researcher's sphere of influence and responsibility.

Some researchers, such as Laura Ellingson (2017), Sarah Pink (2009) and Dawn Lyon (2019) ask us to pay attention to our embodied feelings and sensations and to those of our participants when we conduct research. A focus on emotions is inherently an embodied approach. This understanding of embodiment that looks to include the feelings, movements, images, thoughts and sensations of the body and mind (Leigh and Bailey, 2013) is more holistic, philosophical and, potentially, a less theoretical one. In some of the chapters in this book there is a focus on these 'somatic' approaches, a word first brought into use in this way by Thomas Hanna (1988). A somatic approach to embodiment does not work from the premise that there is a mind/body split, and, instead, sees our 'intelligence seeded in the flesh' (Lakoff and Johnson, 2003). This perspective is influenced by practices of somatic bodywork and its use within therapeutic and educational contexts (Hartley, 2004), and as such, whilst centring the experiences of the participant (or client), holds space and allows for the experiences of the researcher (or practitioner). This way of being embodied asks us to become 'consciously self-aware' (Leigh and Bailey, 2013) and pay attention to ourselves and to others. This aspect of Embodied Inquiry is one that can be present at any stage of any research project or throughout the entire corporeal experience of being an academic (Norgard and Aaen, 2019) – whether it has explicit research questions that relate to embodied ideas, or whether it is a state of mind (and body) of the researcher on a science project or anything in between.

By becoming consciously self-aware it is possible to bring the unconscious emotions and feelings up into consciousness and articulate them. As researchers we can access deeper levels of experience, and are more likely to touch on honest stories rather than those that we consciously want to project onto others. Whilst similar to philosophical ideas such as phenomenology (see Merleau-Ponty, 2002; and Leder, 1990, for example), this approach can be less theoretical and more grounded in the body. In a somatic understanding of embodiment, movement bridges the gap between the body and the mind, allowing us access to the thoughts, feelings, emotions, images and sensations that we experience through all of our awareness (Juhan, 1987). We have spoken a lot about the importance of movement in Embodied Inquiry, and used examples that incorporated Authentic Movement and dance. Movement is fundamental to embodied experience. Both in the larger sense of the 'mobilities' of individuals and peoples (Urry, 2007), and on the micro-scale, that from the smallest cell movement to the largest gesture, there is movement in everything that we do (Chaiklin, 2009). In this book we have focused on movement approaches that are familiar to us, namely Authentic Movement, somatics and yoga, and we have demonstrated how we have used these to inform research and analytic processes. However, as we indicated in Chapter 2, there are many movement forms and bodywork practices that can feed into Embodied Inquiry. Most bodywork practices involve 'hands-on' work or touch. The use of touch, and the significance of human touch on the skin, has long been recognized as important both to our psyche and within language (Montagu, 1971): 'Touch is "chief" amongst the language of our senses' (Westland, 2011, p. 21), and is 'intrinsic to communication' (Westland, 2011, p. 25). Movement and bodywork practices like the ones in Chapter 2 can help us to 'tune in' to what we are doing and feeling. If we think back to Nicole's reflections in Chapter 5, she discussed the challenges of putting this into practice, particularly when we are constrained by language. The connection with language is important (Sheets-Johnstone, 2009), as within Embodied Inquiry there is often an importance placed on the expression, in language, of experience (Fogel, 2009). If a moment is significant, we call it 'touching'; if a person is irritable, we call them 'touchy'. 'Feelings' refer to emotions, and someone who is 'unfeeling' could be referred to as 'callous', which originates from the Latin *callum*, meaning hard skin. Being thin- or thick-skinned, again, implies a judgement on emotional capacity, and to be 'tactful' is to have a sense of what is right when dealing with other people. Embodied Inquiry is not limited to elite movers and athletes. The principles are inclusive, as even if we understand movement to be the bridge between the body and mind, 'movement' does not have to equate to elite activity, nor even gross physical movement. We are all moving all the time as we breathe, as our hearts beat, our lymph moves, our synapses fire and we articulate our thoughts. The impact of this can be seen in collections such as Brown and Leigh's on ableism in academia (2020), where, though embodiment was not an explicit aim of the book, the majority of contributors focused or highlighted embodied experience in order to contextualize their experiences.

Whichever background you are from, or theoretical frame you use, an embodied perspective allows room for a researcher to encompass any of the others. For example, Embodied Inquiry can consider what might appear to be conventional sociological topics. A sociological Embodied Inquiry might be concerned with the clothes that are worn for particular events and how you as researcher, or your participants, react to them, or how weight loss and perceptions of weight play out in society in different contexts and the like. Clothes and appearance are often associated with class, age and gender. For example, when attending a yoga class, noting how often students begin to dress in the same style as their teachers, portraying their identity and understanding of what it means to 'be' in that class; how clubs use uniforms to make and keep a sense of community and belonging; or how the clothes people wear when they are depressed are different from the clothes they wear when they are happy. Embodied Inquiry would be interested in the clothes people wear whilst remaining alert to your own choices, how your own clothes make you feel and how you react to the clothes of others.

An understanding of Embodied Inquiry allows an extra layer of depth to be added to a more theoretical enquiry. This depth might be access to the emotion work that we as researchers or our participants might do. It might be a heightened awareness of our positionality and reflexivity as researchers, and recognizing our own reactions and responses as we move through the process of research design, data collection, analysis and dissemination. It might be a multimodal (Jewitt et al., 2016) approach to data collection itself as a ceremony (Wilson, 2008) and recognizing that capturing experience is a multidimensional act that can reach beyond the text or words that are used to describe it. It might be a focus on the ability our data can have to evoke experience and haunt (Wilson, 2018) our audience. It might be participatory, historical (VariAbilities, 2018), document-based (Grant, 2018a) or autoethnographic (Bochner and Ellis, 2016). Embodied Inquiry is a form of qualitative research that allows space for the embodied experience of the researcher and/or the researched.

Concluding Thoughts

As we showed throughout the book, by acknowledging and centring Embodied Inquiry to the research design approach, Embodied Inquiry can be used to access rich emotional data in order to capture truthful, honest and thick descriptive qualitative data. However, we are very aware that the kinds of examples we have provided are heavily reliant on a Western-centred world view. We stated in Chapter 1 that this book has been shaped by our own experiences and research work, and we cannot deny our personal backgrounds and experience. We are, nevertheless, aware of the many possibilities and potential for Embodied Inquiry, some of which we ourselves are actively pursuing already.

To enquire is to ask, request information, to look into (dictionary ref   http://www.future-perfect.co.uk/grammar-tip/is-it-enquiry-or -inquiry/). An inquiry implies a more specific investigation, and in this case would mean that we are conducting a specific investigation, or part of a specific investigation in an embodied manner. Embodied Inquiry supposes interest in the embodied nature of a thing. That interest might inform all or part of the research design, the data collection, the data analysis or dissemination.

We came to Embodied Inquiry from different starting points. Nicole's background is in education, languages and sociology. Jennifer's is in chemistry, yoga, and somatic movement therapy and education. We are continuing to expand Embodied Inquiry into more areas and disciplines, and a large part of our motivation for writing this book was to bring it to a wider audience. We value Embodied Inquiry for the depth, honesty and richness it brings to any data collection. Further to that, we have witnessed the impact that Embodied Inquiry can have on participants and researchers as they pay attention to and process their hitherto unconscious embodied feelings. Together, we have worked with PhD students, graduate teaching assistants and undergraduate dancers, and brought these methods and ideas to wider audiences through the National Centre for Research Methods, the British Sociological Association, the Society for Research into Higher Education, and international conferences. Separately, Nicole has used creative methods with trainee teachers, and academics with disabilities and chronic illness. Jennifer has worked with teaching staff in Conservatoires, and is working on bringing Embodied Inquiry into the chemical sciences through her work with WISC, an International Network of Women in Supramolecular Chemistry working to support equality and diversity in the chemical sciences.[1] It is our intention to continue to bring this Embodied Inquiry into different disciplines, perhaps working towards an idea of an embodied

---

[1] This is the subject of a forthcoming book provisionally titled *Women in Supramolecular Chemistry* to be published by Bristol University Press by Leigh et al., in 2022.

university (Norgard and Aaen, 2019). Embodied Inquiry is more than just arts, dance or movement-based research. As researchers and participants in research, we find Embodied Inquiry to be a powerful tool to discover and pay attention to the 'dance' – to the fluidity, the expression, the flow – in everything we do (Newlove and Dalby, 2004). Embodied Inquiry incorporates all the unconscious thoughts, feelings, sensations, reflections, emotions and images that arise from and are understood within our bodies and minds. If the approach is reflexive and incorporates an awareness of the body-mind connection, and if the intention is for Embodied Inquiry, then a project set up in this way will realize that ambition.

REFERENCES

@MrMotilalOswal, 2020. *Twitter*. Available at: https://twitter.com/MrMotilalOswal/status/1247669027587018757 (accessed 8 May 2020).

Adler, J. (2002). *Offering from the Conscious Body the Discipline of Authentic Movement*. Rochester, Vermont: Inner Traditions.

Alibali, M. W., and Nathan, M. J. (2012). 'Embodiment in mathematics teaching and learning: Evidence from learners' and teachers' gestures'. *Journal of the Learning Sciences*, 21(2): 247–86.

Allen-Collinson, J., and Owton, H. (2015). 'Intense embodiment: Senses of heat in women's running and boxing'. *Body and Society*, 21(2): 245–68.

Alverson, M., and Skoldberg, K. (2000). *Reflexive Methodology: New Vistas for Qualitative Research*, London: Sage.

Amankwaa, L. (2016). 'Creating protocols for trustworthiness in qualitative research'. *Journal of Cultural Diversity*, 23(3): 121–7.

Anon. (2010). *Practice as Research: Approaches to Creative Arts Enquiry*. London: I.B. Tauris.

Attia, M., and Edge, J. (2017). 'Be(com)ing a reflexive researcher: A developmental approach to research methodology'. *Open Review of Educational Research*, 4(1): 33–45.

Back, L. (2007). *The Art of Listening*. Oxford: Berg.

Bacon, J. (2010). 'The voice of her body: Somatic practices as a basis for creative research methodology'. *Dance and Somatics Journal*, 2(1): 63–74.

Bain, L. (1995). 'Mindfulness and subjective knowledge'. *Quest*, 47, 238–53.

Bainbridge-Cohen, B. (1993). *Sensing, Feeling and Action*. Northampton, MA: Contact Editions.

Barad, K. (2007). *Meeting the Universe Halfway: Quantum Physics and the Entanglement of Matter and Meaning*. Durham, NC: Duke University Press.

Barone, T., and Eisner, E. W. (2012). *Arts Based Research*. Sage.

Barrett, A., Kajamaa, A., and Johnston, J. (2020). 'How to… be reflexive when conducting qualitative research'. *The Clinical Teacher*, 17(1): 9–12.

Barrett, E., and Bolt, B., 2010. *Practice as Research: Approaches to Creative Arts Enquiry*. London: I.B. Tauris.

Bartlett, R. (2015). 'Visualising dementia activism: Using the arts to communicate research findings'. *Qualitative Research*, 15(6): 755–68.

Bartlett, R., and Milligan, C. (2015). *What Is Diary Method?*. London: Bloomsbury Publishing.

Bassey, M. (2000). *Case Study Research in Educational Settings*. Buckingham: Open University Press. Available at: http://www.gbv.de/dms/bowker/toc/9780335199853.pdf (Last accessed August 2019).

Bassey, M. (2001). 'A solution to the problem of generalization in educational research: Empirical findings and fuzzy predictions'. *Oxford Review of Education*, 27(1): 5–22.

Bates, C. (2019). *Vital Bodies: Living with Illness*. Bristol: Policy Press.

Bates, E. A., McCann, J. J., Kaye, L. K., and Taylor, J. C. (2017). '"Beyond words": A researcher's guide to using photo elicitation in psychology'. *Qualitative Research in Psychology*, 4(4): 459–81.

BBC. (April 2019a). *Why I Broke My Non-Disclosure Agreement*. Available at: https://www.bbc.co.uk/news/av/education-47950167/why-i-broke-my-non-disclosure-agreement (Last accessed August 2019).

BBC. (April 2019b). *UK Universities Face 'Gagging Order' Criticism*. Available at: https://www.bbc.co.uk/news/education-47936662 (Last accessed August 2019).

Beck, U., Giddens, A., and Lash, S. (1994). *Reflexive Modernization: Politics, Tradition and Aesthetics in the Modern Social Order*. Stanford University Press.

Becker, H. (1967). 'Whose side are we on?' *Social Problems*, 14(3): 239–47.

Bingham, C. (2010). 'Hermeneutics'. In P. Peterson, E. Baker, and B. McGaw (eds.), *International Encyclopedia of Education*, 3rd edn, New York: Elsevier Science, 63–8.

Birdwhistell, R. L. (1970). *Kinesics and Context: Essays on Body Motion Communication*. Philadelphia: University of Pennsylvania Press.

Birdwhistell, R. L. (1974). 'The language of the body: The natural environment of words'. In A. Silverstein (ed.), *Human Communication: Theoretical Explorations*, 203–20. Routledge.

Bloch, C. (2012). *Passion and Paranoia: Emotions and the Culture of Emotion in Academia*, Abingdon: Routledge.

Bochner, A. and Ellis, C. (2016). *Evocative Autoethnography: Writing Lives and Telling Stories*. London: Routledge.

Bodenhorn, B. (2016). '"What I want is for Florida orange growers to know why it is important for us to whale': Learning to be an anthropologist in the field'. In G. De Neve, and M. Unnithan-Kumar (eds.), *Critical Journeys: The Making of Anthropologists*, 17–30. Routledge.

Bourdieu, P. (1986). 'The forms of capital'. In J. G. Richardson (ed.), *Handbook of Theory and Research for the Sociology of Education*, 241–58.

Bourdieu, P. (2013/1984). *Distinction: A Social Critique of the Judgement of Taste*. Routledge.

Brown, N. and Morgan, C. (2021). 'Rhythmanalysis as a method to account for time in qualitative research'. In B. C. Clift, J. Gore, S. Gustafsson, S. Bekker and I. C. Batlle (eds.), *Temporality in Qualitative Inquiry: Theories, Methods, and Practices*. Routledge.

Bowman, P. (2019). 'Embodiment as embodiment of'. In *Conversations on Embodiment across Higher Education: Teaching, Practice and Research*. Abingdon: Routledge, 11–24.

Bradley, J. (2020). 'Ethnography, arts production and performance: Meaning-making in and for the street'. In T. Lähdesmäki, V. Ceginskas, E. Koskinen-Koivisto, and A.-K. Koistinen (eds.), *Methodological and Ethical Challenges and Solutions in Contemporary Research: Ethnography with a Twist*. Abingdon: Routledge.

Braun, V. and Clarke, V. (2006). 'Using thematic analysis in psychology'. *Qualitative Research in Psychology*, 3(2): 77–101.

Braun, V. and Clarke, V. (2019). 'Reflecting on reflexive thematic analysis'. *Qualitative Research in Sport, Exercise and Health*, 11(4): 589–97.

Braun, V., Clarke, V., Hayfield, N., Frith, H., Malson, H., Moller, N., and Shah-Beckley, I. (2019). 'Qualitative story completion: Possibilities and potential pitfalls'. *Qualitative Research in Psychology*, 16(1): 136–55.

Brew, A., and Lucas, L. (eds.). (2009). *Academic Research and Researchers*. Maidenhead: SRHE and Open University Press.

Brinkmann, S. and Kvale, S. (2015). *InterViews: Learning the Craft of Qualitative Research Interviewing*, 3rd edn. Thousand Oaks CA: SAGE Publications, Inc.

Brookfield, S. (1995). *Becoming a Critically Reflective Teacher*. San-Francisco: Jossey-Bass.

Brown, N. (2017). 'The construction of academic identity under the influence of fibromyalgia'. In: H. Henderson, A. L. Pennant, and M. Hand (eds.), *Papers from the Education Doctoral Research Conference Saturday 26 November 2016: School of Education*, 18–25. Birmingham: University of Birmingham.

Brown, N. (2018a). 'Exploring the lived experience of fibromyalgia using creative data collection'. *Cogent Social Sciences*, 4(1): 1447759.

Brown, N. (2018b). 'Identity boxes: Data collection through objects'. *NCRM Methods News*, 2018(2): 2.

Brown, N. (2019a). '"Listen to your gut": A reflexive approach to data analysis'. *The Qualitative Report*, 24(13): 31–43.

Brown, N. (2019b). 'Identity boxes: using materials and metaphors to elicit experiences'. *International Journal of Social Research Methodology*, 22(5): 487–501.

Brown, N. (2019c). 'Partnership in learning: how staff-student collaboration can innovate teaching'. *European Journal of Teacher Education*, 42(5): 608–20.

Brown, N. (2020). *The 'I' in Fibromyalgia: The Construction of Academic Identity Under the Influence of Fibromyalgia*. (Unpublished doctoral dissertation). University of Kent, Canterbury, UK.

Brown, N. and Collins, J. (2018). 'Using LEGO® to understand emotion work in doctoral education'. *International Journal of Management and Applied Research*, 5(4): 193–209.

Brown, N. and Leigh, J. (2018). 'Creativity and playfulness in HE research'. In J. Huisman and M. Tight (eds.), *Theory and Method in Higher Education Research Volume 4*. Bingley: Emerald.

Brown, N. and Leigh, J. (2020). *Ableism in Academia: Theorising Disabilities and Chronic Illnesses in Higher Education*. London: UCL Press.

Brown, N., Jafferani, A., and Pattharwala, V. (2018). 'Partnership in teacher education: Developing creative methods to deepen students' reflections'. *Journal of Educational Innovation, Partnership and Change*, 4(1). Available at: https://journals.studentengagement.org.uk/index.php/studentchangeagents/article/view/747 (Last accessed 22 January 2021).

Brown, N., Jafferani, A., and Pattharwala, V. (2019). 'Using drawing, model making and metaphorical representations to increase students' engagement with reflections'. *RAISE: Student Engagement in Higher Education Journal*, 2(3): 26–33.

Brown, N. (2021). *How to make the most of your research journal*. Bristol: Policy Press.

Bryman, A. (2016). *Social Research Methods*. Oxford: Oxford University Press.

Buote, V. et al., 2011. 'Setting the bar: Divergent sociocultural norms for women's and men's ideal appearance in real-world contexts'. *Body Image*, 8(4): 322–34.

Butler, J., 1993. *Bodies That Matter: On the Discursive Limits of Sex*. New York: Routledge.

Butler, M., and Derrett, S. (2014). 'The walking interview: An ethnographic approach to understanding disability'. *Internet Journal of Allied Health Sciences and Practice*, 12(3): 6.

Butler-Warke, A. and Hood, C. (2020). *Disposable Humans?*. Available at: https://www.cost-ofliving.net/disposable-humans/?fbclid=IwAR1y8oOgXB9BHffATv7YJfT7Exg3Xp3uJijXB5fIFuCeYdCQND8e_MaG2B4 (accessed 8 May 2020).

Butterfield, L. D., Borgen, W. A., Amundson, N. E., and Maglio, A. S. T. (2005). 'Fifty years of the critical incident technique: 1954–2004 and beyond'. *Qualitative Research*, 5(4): 475–97.

Cacioppo, J., Proester, J. and Berntson, G. (1993). 'Rudimentary derterminants of attitudes. ii: Arm flexion and extension have differential effects on attitudes'. *Journal of Personality and Social Psychology*, 65(1): 5–17.

Chadwick, R. (2017). 'Embodied methodologies: Challenges, reflections and strategies'. *Qualitative Research*, 17(1): 54–74.

Chaiklin, S. (2009). 'We dance from the moment our feet touch the earth'. In S. Chaiklin, and H. Wengrower (eds.), *The Art and Science of Dance / Movement Therapy*, 3–11. Hove: Routledge.

Charmaz, K. (1994, May). 'Identity dilemmas of chronically ill men'. *The Sociological Quarterly*, 35(2): 269–88.

Charmaz, K. (1997). *Good Days, Bad Days: The Self in Chronic Illness and Time*. Rutgers University Press.

Charmaz, K., Harris, S. and Irvine, L. (2019). The Social Self and Everyday Life: Understanding the World through Symbolic Interactionism. Wiley-Blackwell.

Chiseri-Strater, E. (1996). 'Turning in upon ourselves: Positionality, subjectivity, and reflexivity in case study and ethnographic research'. In P. Mortensen, and G. E. Kirsch (eds.), *Ethics and Representation in Qualitative Studies of Literacy*, 115–33. Urbana: NCTE.

Cilley, M. (2002). *Sink Reflections*. New York: Bantam Books.

Clark, A. (2005). 'Listening to and involving young children: A review of research and practice'. *Early Child Development and Care*, 175(6): 489–505.

Clark, A., and Emmel, N. (2010). 'Using walking interviews'. *NCRM – Realities toolkit #13*. Available at: http://www.socialsciences.mancheste r.ac.uk/realities/resources/toolkits/walking-interviews/13-toolkit-wal king-interviews.pdf (Last accessed February 2019).

Clark, A., and Moss, P. (2001). *Listening to Young Children: The Mosaic Approach*. London: National Children's Bureau for the Joseph Rowntree Foundation.

Clarke, V., Hayfield, N., Moller, N., and Tischner, I. (2017). 'Once upon a time…: Story completion methods'. In V. Braun, V. Clarke, and D. Gray (eds.), *Collecting Qualitative Data: A Practical Guide to Textual, Media and Virtual Techniques*, 45–70. Cambridge: Cambridge University Press.

Clough, P. (2002). *Narratives and Fictions in Educational Research*. Maidenhead: Open University Press.

Coad, J. (2007). 'Using art-based techniques in engaging children and young people in health care consultations and/or research'. *Journal of Research in Nursing*, 12(5): 487–97.

Cohen, L., Manion, L., and Morrison, K. (2013). *Research Methods in Education*. Abingdon: Routledge.

'collect, v.'. (n.d.). In *Oxford English Dictionary oed.com*. Available at: https://www.oed.com/view/Entry/36263?rskey=usHANU&result=3#e id (Last accessed April 2020).

Crawford Sheare, N. B. (2008). 'Hair, hands, and oxygen tanks: Embodiment and health empowerment in homebound older women'. *Visions: The Journal of Rogerian Nursing Science*, 15(1): 18–27.

Crenshaw, K., 1989. *Demarginalizing the Intersection of Race and Sex: A Black Feminist Critique of Antidiscrimination Doctrine, Feminist Theory, and Antiracist Politics*, 139–67. Chicago: University of Chicago Legal Forum.

Creswell, J. W., and Miller, D. L. (2000). 'Determining validity in qualitative inquiry'. *Theory into Practice*, 39(3): 124–30.

Csordas, T. (2002). *Body/Meaning/Healing*. Basingstoke: Palgrave Macmillan.

Csordas, T., ed. (1994). *Embodiment and Experience: The Existential Ground of Culture and Soul*. Cambridge: Cambridge University Press.

Cutcliffe, J. R., and Ramcharan, P. (2002). 'Leveling the playing field? Exploring the merits of the ethics-as-process approach for judging qualitative research proposals'. *Qualitative Health Research*, 12(7): 1000–10.

Dahlberg, K., Nyström, M., and Dahlberg, H. (2007). *Reflective Lifeworld Research*. Lund, Sweden: Studentlitteratur.

Darabi, M., Macaskill, A., and Reidy, L. (2016). 'Stress among UK academics: identifying who copes best'. *Journal of Further and Higher Education*. doi:10.1080/0309877X.2015.1117598.

Darawsheh, W., and Stanley, M. (2014). 'Reflexivity in research: Promoting rigour, reliability and validity in qualitative research'. *International Journal of Therapy and Rehabilitation*, 21(12): 560–8.

De Jager, A., Tewson, A., Ludlow, B., and Boydell, K. (2016). 'Embodied ways of storying the self: A systematic review of body-mapping'. *Forum Qualitative Sozialforschung/Forum: Qualitative Social Research*, [S.l.], v. 17(2), may 2016. ISSN 1438-5627. Available at: <http://www.qualitati ve-research.net/index.php/fqs/article/view/2526> (accessed 8 December 2020). doi:http://dx.doi.org/10.17169/fqs-17.2.2526.

Delamont, S. (2018, January). *Truth Is Not Linked to Political Virtue: Problems with Positionality*. Keynote presentation at The Fourth Annual Qualitative Research Symposium, University of Bath, Bath, UK.

Denzin, N. (2003). *Performance Ethnography: Critical Pedagogy and the Politics of Culture*. Thousand Oaks, CA: Sage.

Denzin, N. (2010). *The Qualitative Manifesto*. Abingdon: Routledge.

Denzin, N. K. (2016). *The Qualitative Manifesto: A Call to Arms*. Abingdon: Routledge.

Dockett, S., Einarsdottir, J., and Perry, B. (2017). 'Photo elicitation: Reflecting on multiple sites of meaning'. *International Journal of Early Years Education*, 25(3): 225–40.

Downey, G. (2010). '"Practice without theory": A neuroanthropological perspective on embodied learning'. *Journal of the Royal Anthropological Institute*, S22–40.

Dychtwald, K. (1977). *Bodymind.* New York: Pantheon Books.

Eccleston, C. (2016). *Embodied: The Psychology of Physical Sensation.* Oxford: Oxford University Press.

Edwards, R. (2019). 'I-Poems'. In P. Atkinson, S. Delamont, A. Cernat, J. W. Sakshaug, and R. A. Williams (eds.), *SAGE Research Methods Foundations.* doi: 10.4135/9781526421036745821.

Edwards, R., and Nicoll, K. (2006). 'Expertise, competence and reflection in the rhetoric of professional development'. *British Educational Research Journal*, 32(1): 115–31.

Edwards, R., and Weller, S. (2012). 'Shifting analytic ontology: Using I-poems in qualitative longitudinal research'. *Qualitative Research*, 12(2): 202–17.

Ellingson, L. (2017). *Embodiment in Qualitative Research.* Abingdon: Routledge.

Ellingson, L. L., and Sotirin, P. (2019). 'Data engagement: A critical materialist framework for making data in qualitative research'. *Qualitative Inquiry.* Advance online publication.

Ellingson, L. L., and Sotirin, P. (2020). *Making Data in Qualitative Research: Engagements, Ethics, and Entanglements.* London and New York: Routledge.

Emerson, R. (1995). *Writing Ethnographic Fieldnotes.* Chicago: University of Chicago Press.

Ennals, P., Fortune, T., Williams, A., and D'Cruz, K. (2015). 'Shifting occupational identity: Doing, being, becoming and belonging in the academy'. *Higher Education Research and Development.* doi:10.1080/07294360.2015.1107884.

Erbland, K. (2018). *11 Movies Hot on iPhones.* Available at: https://www.indiewire.com/2018/03/movies-shot-on-iphones-unsane-tangerine-shorts-1201941565/ (accessed 24 May 2020).

Ettorre, E. (2010). 'Autoethnography: Making sense of personal illness journeys'. In I. Bourgeault, R. Dingwall and R. De Vries (eds.), *The SAGE Handbook on Qualitative Methods in Health Research.* London, England: Sage.

Evans, J., and Jones, P. (2011). 'The walking interview: Methodology, mobility and place'. *Applied Geography*, 31(2): 849–58.

Evans, J., Davies, B., and Wright, J., eds. (2004). *Body Knowledge and Control: Studies in the Sociology of Physical Education and Health.* Abingdon: Routledge.

Faulkner, S. L. (2016). *Poetry as Method: Reporting Research through Verse*. Abingdon: Routledge.

Faulkner, S. L. (2018). *Real Women Run: Running as Feminist Embodiment*. Abingdon: Routledge.

Finlay, L. (2015). 'Sensing and making sense: Embodying metaphor in relational-centered psychotherapy'. *The Humanistic Psychologist*, 43(4): 338–53.

Flaherty, C. (2020). *Inside Higher Education*. Available at: https://www.insidehighered.com/news/2020/04/21/early-journal-submission-dat a-suggest-covid-19-tanking-womens-research-productivity (accessed 21 April 2020).

Flanagan, J. C. (1954). 'The critical incident technique'. *Psychological Bulletin*, 51(4): 327.

Flores, E. O. (2016). '"Grow your hair out": Chicano gang masculinity and embodiment in recovery'. *Social Problems*, 63(4): 590–604.

Fogel, A. (2009). *The Psychophysiology of Self-Awareness*. London : Norton.

Foley, D. E. (2002). 'Critical ethnography: The reflexive turn'. *International Journal of Qualitative Studies in Education*, 15(4): 469–90.

Foster, S. L., Laverty-Finch, C., Gizzo, D. P., and Osantowski, J. (1999). 'Practical issues in self-observation'. *Psychological Assessment*, 11(4): 426.

Frank, A. W. (2013). *The Wounded Storyteller: Body, Illness, and Ethics*, 2nd edn. Chicago: University of Chicago Press.

Freedman, D. P., and Stoddard Holmes, M., eds. (2003). *The Teacher's Body: Embodiment, Authority, and Identity in the Academy*. Albany: State University of New York Press.

Frith, H., and Gleeson, K. (2004). 'Clothing and embodiment: Men managing body image and appearance'. *Psychology of Men and Masculinity*, 5(1): 40.

Fryberg, S. and Martinez, E., eds. (2014). *The Truly Diverse Faculty: New Dialogues in American Higher Education*. Basingstoke: Palgrave Macmillan.

Gadamer, H.-G. (2004). *A Century of Philosophy*, trans. R. Koepke, and S. Coltman. New York: Continuum.

Gadamer, H. G. (2006/1975). *Truth and Method*, rev. trans. J. Weinsheimer, and D. G. Marshall. London and New York: Continuum.

Gandhi, M. (1929). *The Gita According to Gandhi*, trans. M. Desai. Ahmedabad: Navajivan Publ. House.

Gauntlett, D. (2007). *Creative Explorations: New Approaches to Identities and Audiences*. Abingdon: Routledge.

'gather, v.'. (n.d.). In *Oxford English Dictionary oed.com*. Available at https://www.oed.com/view/Entry/77077?result=3&rskey=3KRuzH& (Last accessed April 2020).

Geertz, C. (1973). *The Interpretation of Cultures*. New York, NY: Basic

Gibson, W., and Vom Lehn, D. (2020). 'Seeing as accountable action: The interactional accomplishment of sensorial work'. *Current Sociology*, 68(1): 77–96.

Goellner, E., and Murphy, S., eds. (1995). *Bodies of the Text: Dance as Theory, Literature as Dance*. New Brunswick, NJ: Rutgers University Press.

Goffman, A. (2014). *On the Run: Fugitive Life in an American City*. Chicago: University of Chicago Press.

Grant, A. (2016). '"I…don't want to see you flashing your bits around': Exhibitionism, othering, and good motherhood in perceptions of public breastfeeding'. *Geoforum*, 71: 52–61.

Grant, A. (2018). *Doing Excellent Social Research with Documents*. Abingdon: Routledge.

Greenhalgh, T. (@trishgreenhalgh). (2020). *I Enjoyed Writing This Sentence in a Paper*. [Twitter post] Available at: https://twitter.com/trishgreenhalgh/status/1227677353419079680 (accessed April 2020).

Gruenberg, B. (1978). 'The problem of reflexivity in the sociology of science'. *Philosophy of the Social Sciences*, 8(4): 321–43.

Guell, C. and Ogilvie, D. (2015). 'Picturing commuting: Photovoice and seeking well-being in everyday travel'. *Qualitative Research*, 15(2): 201–18.

Gullion, J. S. (2014). *October Birds: A Novel about Pandemic Influenza, Infection Control and First Responders*. Leiden: Brill Sense.

Hagens, C., Beaman, A. and Bouchard, R. E. (2003). 'Reminiscing, poetry writing, and remembering boxes: Person-centred communication with cognitively impaired older adults'. *Activities, Adaptation and Aging*, 27 (3/4): 97–112.

Halstead, N. (2016). 'Others in and of the field: Anthropology and knowledgeable persons'. In G. De Neve, and M. Unnithan-Kumar (eds.), *Critical Journeys: The Making of Anthropologists*, 47–66. Abingdon: Routledge.

Hammersley, M. (2006). 'Ethnography: Problems and prospects'. *Ethnography and Education*, 1(1): 3–14.

Hanna, T. (1988). *Somatics*. s.l.:Da Capo Press.

Harris, A. (2016a). *Video as Method: Understanding Qualitative Research*. Oxford: Oxford University Press.

Harris, J. (2016b). 'Utilizing the walking interview to explore campus climate for students of color'. *Journal of Student Affairs Research and Practice*, 53(4): 365–77.

Hartley, L. (1989). *Wisdom of the Body Moving*. Berkeley, CA: North Atlantic Books.

Hartley, L. (2004). *Somatic Psychology Body, Mind and Meaning*. London: Whurr Publishers.

Harvey, L., McCormick, B., Vanden, K. (2019). 'Becoming at the boundaries of language: Dramatic enquiry for intercultural learning in UK higher education'. *Language and Intercultural Communication*, 19(6): 541–70.

Hay, D., and Pitchford, S. (2016). 'Curating blood: How students' and researchers' drawings bring potential phenomena to light'. *International Journal of Science Education*, 38(17): 2596–620.

Haynes, K. (2012). 'Reflexivity in qualitative research'. In G. Symon, and C. Cassell (eds.), *Qualitative Organizational Research: Core Methods and Current Challenges*, 72–89. London: Sage.

Heath, C. (2002). 'Demonstrative suffering: The gestural (re) embodiment of symptoms'. *Journal of Communication*, 52(3): 597–616.

Heidegger, M. (1996/1953). *Being and Time: A Translation of Sein and Zeit*, trans. J. Stambaugh. New York: State University of New York Press.

Hennink, M., Hutter, I., and Bailey, A. (2020). *Qualitative Research Methods*. London: Sage Publications Limited.

Hesmondhalgh, D., and Baker, S. (2013). *Creative Labour: Media Work in Three Cultural Industries*. Abingdon: Routledge.

Huggins, R. (2016). 'The addict's body: Embodiment, drug use, and representation'. In P. Vannini (ed.), *Body/Embodiment: Symbolic Interaction and the Sociology of the Body*, 165–80. Abingdon, Oxon and New York: Routledge.

Husserl, E. (1927). 'Phenomenology'. *Encyclopaedia Britannica*, rev. trans. R. Palmer. Available at: http://www.metinbal.net/metin_bal_Courses _instructed_by/Course_Texts/Husserls_Phenomenology_Britannica_Ar ticle.pdf (Last accessed April 2020).

Inckle, K. (2009). *Writing on the Body? Thinking through Gendered Embodiment and Marked Flesh*. Cambridge: Cambridge Scholars Publishing.

Irvin, S. (2016). *Body Aesthetics*. Oxford: Oxford University Press.

Irwin, L. and Johnson, J. (2006). 'Interviewing young children: explicating our practices and dilemmas'. *Qualitative Health Research*, 15(6): 821–31.

ISMETA. (n.d.). Retrieved 2010 18-July from http://www.ismeta.org/

Iyengar, B. K. (1966). *Light on Yoga*. London: HarperCollins.

Iyengar, B. K. S. (1993). *Light on the Yoga Sutras of Patanjali*. Glasgow: Caledonian I.B.M. Ltd.

Jagodzinski, J. and Wallin, J. (2013). *Arts-based Research: A Critique and a Proposal*. Rotterdam: Sense.

James, A. (2013). 'Seeking the analytic imagination: Reflections on the process of interpreting qualitative data'. *Qualitative Research*, 13(5): 562–77.

Jewitt, C., Bezemer, J., and O'Halloran, K. (2016). *Introducing Multimodality*. Abingdon: Routledge.

Jivraj, S. (2019). *Decolonise UKC: Through the kaleidoscope*. Available at: https://decoloniseukc.org/about/ (accessed 24 May 2020).

Johnson, D. H. (1995). *Bone, Breath and Gesture*. Berkeley, CA: North Atlantic Books.

Jones, K. (2012). *Rufus Stone*. Available at: https://vimeo.com/109360805 (Last accessed April 2020).

Jones, K. (2013). *Research as Fiction: 'The Return of Rufus Stone' by Kip Jones*. Available at: https://microsites.bournemouth.ac.uk/rufus-stone /2013/12/23/research-as-fiction-the-return-of-rufus-stone-by-kip-jones/ (Last accessed April 2020).

Jones, P., Bunce, G., Evans, J., Gibbs, H., and Hein, J. R. (2008). 'Exploring space and place with walking interviews'. *Journal of Research Practice*, 4(2): D2.

Jordan, S. A. (2001). 'Writing the other, writing the self: Transforming consciousness through ethnographic writing'. *Language and Intercultural Communication*, 1(1): 40–56.

Juhan, D. (1987). *Job's Body*. Barrytown, NY: Station Hill Press.

Kara, H. (2015). *Creative Research Methods in the Social Sciences: A Practical Guide*. Bristol: Policy Press.

Kara, H. (2018). *Research Ethics in the Real World: Euro-Western and Indigenous Perspectives*. Bristol: Policy Press.

Kelley, A., Belcourt-Dittloff, A., Belcourt, C., and Belcourt, G. (2013). 'Research ethics and indigenous communities'. *American Journal of Public Health*, 103(12): 2146–52.

King, V. (2013). 'Self-portrait with mortar board: A study of academic identity using the map, the novel and the grid'. *Higher Education Research and Development*, 32(1): 96–108.

Kitzinger, C., and Powell, D. (1995). 'Engendering infidelity: Essentialist and social constructionist readings of a story completion task'. *Feminism and Psychology*, 5(3): 345–72.

Koelsch, L. E. (2015). 'I poems: Evoking self'. *Qualitative Psychology*, 2(1): 96.

Kolb, D. (1984). *Experiential Learning: Experience as the Source of Learning and Development*. Eaglewood Cliffs, NJ: Prentice Hall.

Lakoff, G. and Johnson, M. (2003). *Metaphors We Live By*, 2 edn. Chicago: University of Chicago Press.

Lamb, G. S., and Huttlinger, K. (1989). 'Reflexivity in nursing research'. *Western Journal of Nursing Research*, 11(6): 765–72.

Langer, P. C. (2016). 'The research vignette: Reflexive writing as interpretative representation of qualitative inquiry—A methodological proposition'. *Qualitative Inquiry*, 22(9): 735–44.

Leader, K. (2015). 'Stories on the skin: Tattoo culture at a South Florida university. *Arts and Humanities in Higher Education*, 14(4): 426–46.

Leader, K. (2016). '"On the book of my body": Women, power, and tattoo culture'. *Feminist Formations*, 28(3): 174–95.

Leavy, P. (2015). *Method Meets Art: Arts-Based Research Practice*, 2nd edn. Guildford: Guilford Publications.

Leavy, P. (2016). *Fiction as Research Practice: Short Stories, Novellas, and Novels*. Abingdon: Routledge.

Leavy, P. (2020). *The Candy Floss Collection: Three Novels*. Boston: Brill Sense.

Leder, D. (1990). *The Absent Body*. Chicago, IL: University of Chicago Press.

Lefevbre, H. (2004). *Rhythmanalysis: Space, Time and Everyday Life*. London: Continuum.

Leigh, A. (1998). *Referral and Termination Issues for Counsellors*. London: Sage.

Leigh, Blackburn and Brown (2018). '*Thoughts on something*' a screened at Disrupticon (London). https://vimeo.com/250364867.

Leigh, J. and Bailey, R. (2013). 'Reflection, reflective practice and embodied reflective practice'. *Body, Movement and Dance in Psychotherapy*, 8(3): 160–71.

Leigh, J., and Blackburn, C. A. (Directors). (2017). *Exploring Embodied Academic Identity through Creative Research Methods* [Motion Picture]. Retrieved from https://vimeo.com/245602322.

Leigh, J. (2012). *Somatic Movement and Education: A Phenomenological Study of Young Children's Perceptions, Expressions and Reflections of Embodiment through Movement*, s.l.: Ph.D. Thesis, University of Birmingham.

Leigh, J. (2018). *SRHE Final Project Report: Exploring Embodied Academic Identity*. Available at: https://www.srhe.ac.uk/downloads/reports-2016/LEIGH-Jennifer-SRHE-NR-Final-Report.pdf (accessed 14 May 2020).

Leigh, J., ed. (2019a). *Conversations on Embodiment across Higher Education: Research, Teaching and Practice*. Abingdon: Routledge.

Leigh, J. (2019b). 'Embodied practice and embodied academic identity'. In J. Leigh (ed.), *Conversations on Embodiment across Higher Education: Teaching, Practice and Research*, 151–70. Abingdon: Routledge.

Leigh, J. (2019c). 'An embodied approach in a cognitive discipline'. In *Educational Futures and Fractures*. London: Palgrave.

Leigh, J. (2020a). 'What would a longitudinal rhythmanalysis of a qualitative researcher's life look like?' In *Temporality in Qualitative Inquiry: Theory, Methods, and Practices*. Abingdon: Routledge.

Leigh, J. (2020b). 'Using creative research methods and movement to encourage reflection in children'. *Journal of Early Childhood Research*, 18(2): 130–42.

Leigh, J. (2023). *Boundaries of Qualitative Research: Between Research, Therapy, Art, and Science*. Bristol: Bristol University Press.

Leigh, J., Hiscock, J., Haynes, C., McConnell, A., Draper, E., Kieffer, M., Hutchins, K., Watkins, D., Caltagirone, C., and Slater, A. (2022). *Women in Supramolecular Chemistry*. Bristol: Bristol University Press.

Lepecki, A., ed. (2004). *Of the Presence of the Body: Essays on Dance and Performance Theory*. Middletown, CT: Wesleyan University Press.

Lewis, N. M. (2017). 'Linked life courses in fieldwork: Researcher, participant and field'. *Area*, 49(4): 394–401.

Lichtman, M. (2012). *Qualitative Research in Education: A User's Guide*. Sage Publications.

Lincoln, Y. S., and Guba, E. G. (1990). 'Judging the quality of case study reports'. *International Journal of Qualitative Studies in Education*, 3(1): 53–9.

Long, T., and Johnson, M. (2000). 'Rigour, reliability and validity in qualitative research'. *Clinical Effectiveness in Nursing*, 4(1): 30–7.

Lury, C., and Wakeford, N., eds. (2012). *Inventive Methods: The Happening of the Social*. Abingdon: Routledge.

Lyon, D. (2016). 'Researching young people's orientations to the future: The methodological challenges of using arts practice. *Qualitative Research*, 16(4): 430–45.

Lyon, D. (2019). *What Is Rhythmanalysis?* London: Bloomsbury.

Lyon, D. and Back, L. (2012). 'Fishmongers in a global economy: Craft and social relations on a London market'. *Sociological Research Online*, 17(2): 1–11.

MacLure, M. (2003). *Discourse in Educational and Social Research*. Buckingham: Open University Press.

MacLure, M. (2011). 'Qualitative inquiry: Where are the ruins?'. *Qualitative Inquiry*, 17(10): 997–1005.

Macmillan. (2014). '*Making a memory box*' at *www.nhs.uk*. Available at: http://www.nhs.uk/ipgmedia/National/Macmillan%20Cancer%20Sup port/assets/MemoryboxMCS4pages.pdf (Last accessed December 2016).

Malcolm, J., and Zukas, M. (2009). 'Making a mess of academic work: Experience, purpose and identity'. *Teaching in Higher Education*, 14(5): 495–506.

Manderson, L. (2005). 'Boundary breaches: The body, sex and sexuality after stoma surgery'. *Social Science & Medicine*, 61(2): 405–15.

Mannay, D., and Staples, E. (2019). '13| Sandboxes, stickers and superheroes'. In D. Mannay, A. Rees, and L. Roberts (eds.), *Children and Young People 'Looked After'?: Education, Intervention and the Everyday Culture of Care in Wales*, Cardiff: University of Wales Press, 169–182.

Mannay, D., Staples, E., and Edwards, V. (2017). 'Visual methodologies, sand and psychoanalysis: Employing creative participatory techniques to explore the educational experiences of mature students and children in care'. *Visual Studies*, 32(4): 345–58.

Mason, J. and Davies, K. (2009). 'Coming to our senses? A critical approach to sensory methodology'. *Qualitative Research*, 9(5): 587–603.

Mauthner, M. (1997). 'Methodological aspects of collecting data from children: Lessons frm three research projects. *Children and Society*, 11: 16–28.

McCabe, M., de Waal Malefyt, T., and Fabri, A. (2017). 'Women, makeup, and authenticity: Negotiating embodiment and discourses of beauty'. *Journal of Consumer Culture*, 1469540517736558: 656–677.

McCormack, D. (2013). *Refrains for Moving Bodies: Experience and Experiment in Affective Spaces*. Durham: Duke University Press.

McDonald, L., Glen, F. C., Taylor, D. J., and Crabb, D. P. (2017). 'Self-monitoring symptoms in glaucoma: A feasibility study of a web-based diary tool'. *Journal of Ophthalmology*, 2017, Article ID 8452840, 8 pages, 2017. https://doi.org/10.1155/2017/8452840.

McMahon, J. and DinanThompson, M. (2011). 'Body work—regulation of a swimmer body': An autoethnography from an Australian elite swimmer'. *Sport, Education and Society*, 16(1): 35–50.

Merleau-Ponty, M. (2002). *Phenomenology of Perception*. Oxon: Routledge.

Mewburn, I. (2012). *Doctorates Down Under: Keys to Successful Doctoral Study in Australia and Aotearoa, New Zealand*, 2nd edn. Australian Council for Educational Research Press.

Mills, C. W. (1959). *Sociological Imagination and the Power Elite*. New York: Oxford University Press.

Morash, K. (2018). An investigation into how engagement with the context and processes of collaborative devising affects the praxis of the playwright: A practice as research PhD. Goldsmiths, University of London.

Montagu, A. (1971). *Touching the Human Significance of Skin*. London: Harper & Row.

Morgan, D. L. (2018). 'Themes, theories, and models'. *Qualitative Health Research*, 28(3): 339–45.

Morse, J. M., Barrett, M., Mayan, M., Olson, K., and Spiers, J. (2002). 'Verification strategies for establishing reliability and validity in qualitative research'. *International Journal of Qualitative Methods*, 1(2): 13–22.

Newlove, J. and Dalby, J. (2004). *Laban for All*. London: NickHern Books.

NICE. (2009). *Promoting Mental Well-Being through Productive and Health Working Conditions: Guidance for Employees*. Promoting mental well-being at work: Nice Public health guidance 22.

Nind, M., and Vinha, H. (2016). 'Creative interactions with data: Using visual and metaphorical devices in repeated focus groups'. *Qualitative Research*, 16(1): 9–26.

Nolan, B. A. D., Mathews, R. M., and Harrison, M. (2001). 'Using external memory aids to increase room finding by older adults with dementia'. *American Journal of Alzheimer's Disease and Other Dementias*, 16(4): 251–4.

Norgard, R. T., and Aaen, J. (2019). 'A university for the body: On the corporeal being of academic existence'. In S. Bengsten and R. Barnett (eds.), *Philosophy and Theory in Higher Education*, 175–99. New York: Peter Lang.

Oakley, A. (1981). 'Interviewing women: A contradiction in terms'. In H. Roberts (ed.), *Doing Feminist Research*, 30–61. London: Routledge.

Oakley, A. (2007). *Fracture: Adventures of a Broken Body*. Bristol: Policy Press.

O'Loughlin, M. (2006). *Embodiment and Education: Exploring Creatural Existence*. Dordrecht: Springer.

Orr, N. and Phoenix, C. (2015). 'Photographing physical activity: Using visual methods to "grasp at" the sensual experiences of the ageing body'. *Qualitative Research*, 15(4): 454–72.

Owens, E., and Beistle, B. (2016). 'Eating the black body: Interracial desire, food metaphor and white fear'. In P. Vannini (ed.), *Body/Embodiment: Symbolic Interaction and the Sociology of the Body*, 201–12. Abingdon, Oxon and New York: Routledge.

Panter, M. (2020). *The Ethics of Manuscript Authorship: Best Practices for Attribution*. Available at: https://www.aje.com/en/arc/ethics-manuscript-authorship/ (accessed 24 May 2020).

Payne, G. and Payne, J. (2004). *Key Concepts in Social Research*. London: Sage.

Petsilas, P., Leigh, J., Brown, N., and Blackburn, C. (2019a). 'Creative and embodied methods to teach reflections and support students' learning'. *Research in Dance Education*, 20(1): 19–35, DOI: 10.1080/14647893.2019.1572733.

Petsilas, P., Leigh, J., Brown, N., and Blackburn, C. (2019b). 'Embodied reflection: Exploring creative routes to teaching reflective practice within dance training'. *Journal of Dance & Somatic Practices*, 11(2): 177–195.

Pezalla, A. E., Pettigrew, J., and Miller-Day, M. (2012). 'Researching the researcher-as-instrument: An exercise in interviewer self-reflexivity'. *Qualitative Research*, 12(2): 165–85.

Piaget, J. (1953/2011). *The Origin of Intelligence in the Child (Jean Piaget: Selected Works)*. Abingdon, UK: Routledge.

Pickard, A. (2007). 'Girls, bodies and pain: Negotiating the body in ballet'. In I. Wellard (ed.), *Rethinking Gender and Youth Sport*, 8–50. London: Routledge.

Pink, S. (2009). *Doing Sensory Ethnography*. London: Sage.

Pink, S. (2015). *Doing Visual Ethnography*, 2nd edn. London: Sage.

Plato (2009). *Phaedo*. Oxford: Oxford Paperbacks trans. Gallop D

Ponty (2005/1962); should this be Merleau-Ponty, M. (2002). *Phenomenology of Perception*. Oxon: Routledge.

Postma, M., and Crawford, P. (2006). *Reflecting Visual Ethnography: Using the Camera in Anthropological Research*. Michigan: CNWS Publications.

Preiser, S. (2006). 'Creativity research in German-speaking countries'. In J. C. Kaufman and R. J. Sternberg (eds.), *The International Handbook of Creativity*. Cambridge University Press, 167–201.

Prendergast, M. (2006). 'Found poetry as literature review: Research poems on audience and performance'. *Qualitative Inquiry*, 12(2): 369–88.

Prichard, I., and Tiggemann, M. (2008). 'Relations among exercise type, self-objectification, and body image in the fitness centre environment: The role of reasons for exercise'. *Psychology of Sport and Exercise*, 9(6): 855–66.

Rajan-Rankin, S. (2018). 'Invisible bodies and disembodied voices? Identity work, the body and embodiment in transnational service work'. *Gender Work and Organization*, 25: 9–23.

Ramcharan, P., and Cutcliffe, J. R. (2001). 'Judging the ethics of qualitative research: Considering the "ethics as process" model'. *Health & Social Care in the Community*, 9(6): 358–66.

Rapport, F., ed. (2004). *New Qualitative Methodologies in Health and Social Care Research*. Abingdon: Routledge.

Richardson, L. (2000). 'Writing: A method of inquiry'. In N. Denzin and Y. Lincoln (eds.), *The SAGE Handbook of Qualitative Research*, 2nd edn, 923–43. Thousand Oaks, CA: SAGE.

Richardson, L. (2003). 'Writing: A method of inquiry'. In Y. Lincoln and N. Denzin (eds.), *Turning Points in Qualitative Research: Tying Knots in a Handkerchief*, 379–96. Walnut Creek, CA: Altamira.

Richardson, L. (2020). *Lone Twin: A True Story of Loss and Found*. Boston: Brill Sense.

Rodriguez, N. M., Ryave, A., and Ryave, A. L. (2002). *Systematic Self-observation: A Method for Researching the Hidden and Elusive Features of Everyday Social Life*, Vol. 49. London: Sage.

Rogers, C. A. (1967). *A Therapist's View of Psychotherapy*. London: Constable.

Rosen, R. (2002). *The Yoga of Breath*. Boston: Shambhala Publications.

Rubenfeld, I. (1977). 'Interview with Irmgard Bertenieff'. *Somatics*, 9–13.

Rufus Stone. (n.d.). *Rufus Stone – A Film About Love, Sexual Awakening and Treachery*. Available at: https://microsites.bournemouth.ac.uk/rufus-stone/ (Last accessed April 2020).

Runco, M. A. and Jaeger, G. J. (2012). 'The standard definition of creativity'. *Creativity Research Journal*, 24(1): 92–6.

Rutakumwa, R., Mugisha, J. O., Bernays, S., Kabunga, E., Tumwekwase, G., Mbonye, M., and Seeley, J. (2019). 'Conducting in-depth interviews with and without voice recorders: A comparative analysis'. *Qualitative Research*. 1468794119884806.

Saldaña, J. (1999). 'Playwriting with data: Ethnographic performance texts'. *Youth Theatre Journal*, 13(1): 60–71.

Saldaña, J. (2015). *Thinking Qualitatively: Methods of Mind*. London: Sage.

Saldaña, J., and Omasta, M. (2016). *Qualitative Research: Analyzing Life*. London: Sage.

Salmenius-Suominen, H., Lehtovirta, M., Vepsäläinen, H., Konttinen, H., and Erkkola, M. (2016). 'Visual Food Diary for Social Support, Dietary Changes and Weight Loss'. *Iproceedings*, 2(1): e38.

Sandelowski, M. (1994). 'The proof is in the pottery: Toward a poetic for qualitative inquiry'. In J. M. Morse (ed.), *Critical Issues in Qualitative Research Methods*. Sage, 46–63.

Savin-Baden, M. S. and Wimpenny, K. (2014). *A Practical Guide to Arts-Related Research*. London: Springer.

Scarry, E. (1985). *The Body in Pain: the Making and Unmaking of the World*. Oxford: Oxford University Press.

Schiffmann, E. (1996). *Yoga: The Spirit and Practice of Moving into Stillness*. New York: Pocket Books.

Schipper, K., Abma, T. A., van Zadelhoff, E., van de Griendt, J., Nierse, C., and Widdershoven, G. A. (2010). 'What does it mean to be a patient research partner? An ethnodrama'. *Qualitative Inquiry*, 16(6): 501–10.

Shakespeare, P., Atkinson, D., and French, S., eds. (1993). *Reflecting on Research Practice: Issues in Health and Social Welfare*. Buckingham: Open University Press.

Sheets-Johnstone, M. (2009). *The Corporeal Turn: An Interdisciplinary Reader*. London: Imprint Academic.

Sheets-Johnstone, M. (2010). 'Kinesthetic experience: Understanding movement inside and out'. *Body, Movement and Dance in Psychotherapy*, 5(2): 111–27.

Shelton, S., Flynn, J., and Grosland, T., eds. (2018). *Feminism and Intersectionality in Academia: Women's Narratives and Experiences in Higher Education*. Basingstoke: Palgrave Macmillan.

Sherwood, J. (2013). 'An Aboriginal health worker's research story'. In D. Mertens, F. Cram, and B. Chilisa (eds.), *Indigenous Pathways into Social Research: Voices of a New Generation*, 203–17. Walnut Creek, CA: Left Coast Press.

Shilling, C. (2012). *The Body and Social Theory*. London: Sage.

Siddique, H., Cvorak, M., Chulani, N., and Lamborn, K. (2020). 'Why BAME people may be more at risk from coronavirus'. *The Guardian*, 1 May, https://www.theguardian.com/world/video/2020/may/01/why -bame-people-may-be-more-at-risk-from-coronavirus-video-explainer.

Silverman, D. (2015). *Interpreting Qualitative Data*. London: Sage.

Smith, J., ed. (2008). *Qualitative Psychology: A Practical Guide to Research Methods*. London: Sage.

Smith, B., and McGannon, K. R. (2018). 'Developing rigor in qualitative research: Problems and opportunities within sport and exercise psychology'. *International Review of Sport and Exercise Psychology*, 11(1): 101–21.

Smith, J. A., Flowers, P., and Larkin, M. (2012). *Interpretative Phenomenological Analysis: Theory, Method and Research*. London: Sage.

Snowber, C. (2016). *Embodied Inquiry: Writing, Living and Being Through the Body*. Rotterdam: Sense.

Sommers, J., and Drake, A. (2006). *The Joseph Cornell Box: Found Objects, Magical Worlds*. Kennerbunkport, ME: Cider Mill Press.

Sontag, S. (2003). *Regarding the Pain of Others*. London: Penguin Books.

Spatz, B. (2015). *What a Body Can Do: Technique as Knowledge, Practice as Research*. Abingdon: Routledge.

Spatz, B. (2020). *Blue Sky Body: Thresholds for Embodied Research*. Abingdon: Routledge.

Spatz, B. (forthcoming). *Making a Laboratory: Dynamic Configurations with Transversal Video*. Brooklyn, NY: Punctum Books.

Stahl, B. (2011). 'Teaching ethical reflexivity in information systems: How to equip students to deal with moral and ethical issues of emerging information and communication technologies'. *Journal of Information Systems*, 22(3): 253–60.

Tarozzi, M. (2020). *What is Grounded Theory?* London: Bloomsbury.

Tarr, J., and Thomas, H. (2011). 'Mapping embodiment: Methodologies for representing pain and injury'. *Qualitative Research*, 11(2): 147–57.

Tarr, J., Gonzalez-Polledo, E., and Cornish, F. (2018). 'On liveness: Using arts workshops as a research method'. *Qualitative Research*, 18(1): 36–52.

Taylor, C., and Bradshaw, E. (2013). 'Tied to the toilet: lived experiences of altered bowel function (anterior resection syndrome) after temporary stoma reversal'. *Journal of Wound Ostomy & Continence Nursing*, 40(4): 415–21.

Taylor, C., and Morgan, L. (2011). 'Quality of life following reversal of temporary stoma after rectal cancer treatment'. *European Journal of Oncology Nursing*, 15(1): 59–66.

Thapan, M. (2004). 'Embodiment and identity in contemporary society: Femina and the "new" Indian woman'. *Contributions to Indian Sociology*, 38(3): 411–44.

The Healer and the Psychiatrist. 2019. Directed by Mike Poltorak. UK: Potolahi Productions in association with the School of Anthropology and Conservation, University of Kent.

Thomas, D. (2020). *Democracy, Diversity and Decolonisation: Staff-student Partnerships in a Reading List Review*. Available at: https://www.advance-he.ac.uk/news-and-views/Democracy-Diversity-and-Decolonisation (accessed 8 May 2020).

Thomas, H., and Tarr, J. (2009). 'Dancers' experiences of pain and injury: Positive and negative effects'. *Journal for Dance Medicine and Science*, 13(2): 51–9.

Thorburn, M. (2008). 'Articulating a Merleau-Pontian phenomenology of physical education: The quest for active student engagement and authentic assessment in high-stakes examination awards'. *European Physical Education Review*, 14(2): 263–80.

Thorpe, G., Arthur, A., and McArthur, M. (2016). 'Adjusting to bodily change following stoma formation: A phenomenological study'. *Disability and Rehabilitation*, 38(18): 1791–802.

Tracy, S. J. (2010). 'Qualitative quality: Eight "big-tent" criteria for excellent qualitative research'. *Qualitative Inquiry*, 16(10): 837–51.

Tremmel, R. (1993). 'Zen and the art of reflective practice in teacher education'. *Harvard Educational Review*, 63(4): 434–58.

Trimingham, M. (2002). 'A methodology for practice as research'. *Studies in Theatre Performance*, 22(1): 54–60.

Urry, J. (2007). *Mobilities*. Bristol: Polity.

van den Scott, L. J. K. (2018). 'Role transitions in the field and reflexivity: From friend to researcher'. In T. Loughran and D. Mannay (eds.), *Emotion and the Researcher: Sites, Subjectivities, and Relationships (Studies in Qualitative Methodology, Volume 16)*. Emerald Publishing Limited, 19–32.

Vannini, P. (2016). *Body/Embodiment: Symbolic Interaction and the Sociology of the Body*. Abingdon: Routledge.

Varela, F., Thompson, E., and Rosch, E. (1993). *The Embodied Mind: Cognitive Science and Human Experience*. Cambridge, MA: MIT Press.

VariAbilities, 2018. *VariAbilities Queerbodies Peculiarbodies*. Available at: https://peculiarbodies.org/variabilities/ (accessed 26 May 2020).

Virtbauer, G. (2016). 'Presencing process: Embodiment and healing in the Buddhist practice of mindfulness of breathing'. *Mental Health, Religion and Culture*, 19(1): 68–81.

Vishnu-devanander, S. (1997). *Hatha Yoga Pradipika*. New York, NY: Om Lotus.

Wacquant, L. (2004). *Body and Soul: Ethnographic Notebooks of an Apprentice-boxer*. New York: Oxford University Press.

Waldman, D. (2002). *Joseph Cornell: Master of Dreams*. Harry N Abrams Incorporated.

Walker, S., Read, S., and Priest, H. (2013). 'Use of reflexivity in a mixed-methods study'. *Nurse Researcher*, 20(3): 38–43.

Walliman, N. (2017). *Research Methods: The Basics*. Abingdon: Routledge.

Warren, S. (2017). 'Pluralising the walking interview: Researching (im) mobilities with Muslim women'. *Social & Cultural Geography*, 18(6): 786–807.

Watson, B. and Leigh, J. (2021). 'Using photo diaries as an inclusive method to explore information experiences in Higher Education'. In *Exploring diary methods in higher education research: Opportunities, Choices and Challenges – Research into Higher Education*. Xuemeng Cao & Emily Henderson Abingdon: Routledge.

Watts, A. (1957). *The Way of Zen*. New York: Vintage Books.

Watts, A. (1961). *Psychotherapy East and West*. New York: Random House.

Weiss, H. (2009). 'The use of mindfulness in psychodynamic and body orientated psychotherapy'. *Body, Movement and Dance in Psychotherapy*, 4(1): 5–16.

Weiss, G. (2013). *Body Images: Embodiment as Intercorporeality*. Abingdon: Routledge.

Westfall, R. (2016). 'The pregnant/birthing body: Negotiations of personal autonomy'. In P. Vannini (ed.), *Body/Embodiment: Symbolic Interaction and the Sociology of the Body*, 263–76. Abingdon, Oxon and New York: Routledge.

Westland, G. (2011). 'Physical touch in psychotherapy: Why are we not touching more?' *Body, Movement and Dance in Psychotherapy*, 6(1): 17–19.

White, K., and Harth, M. (2001). 'Classification, epidemiology, and natural history of fibromyalgia'. *Current Pain and Headache Reports*, 5: 320–9.

Whitehouse, M. (1995). 'The Tao of the body'. In D. H. Johnson (ed.), *Bone, Breath, and Gesture*, 239–51. Berkeley, CA: North Atlantic Books.

Whitty, M. T. (2005). 'The realness of cybercheating: Men's and women's representations of unfaithful Internet relationships'. *Social Science Computer Review*, 23(1): 57–67.

Wilson, S. (2008). *Research Is Ceremony: Indigenous Research Methods*. Halifax and Winnipeg: Fernwood Publishing.

Wilson, S. (2018). 'Haunting and the knowing and showing of qualitative research'. *The Sociological Review*, 66(6): 1209–25.

Wolfe, F., Clauw, D. J., Fitzcharles, M. A., Goldenberg, D. L., Katz, R. S., Mease, P., Russell, A. S., Russell, I. J., Winfield, J. B., and Yunus, M. B. (2010). 'The American College of Rheumatology preliminary diagnostic criteria for fibromyalgia and measurement of symptom severity'. *Arthritis Care and Research*, 62(5): 600–10.

Wood, E. (1959). *Yoga*. Middlesex: Penguin.

Xenitidou, M., and Gilbert, N. (2012). 'The processes of methodological innovation narrative accounts and reflections'. *Methodological Innovations*, 7(1): 1–6.

Yardley, L. (1999). 'Understanding embodied experience'. In Michael Murray and Jerry Chamberlain (eds.), *Qualitative Health Psychology Theories and Methods*, 31–46, London: Sage.

Zimmermann, J. (2015). *Hermeneutics: A Very Short Introduction*. Oxford: Oxford University Press.

Zuesse, E. (1985). 'The role of intentionality in the phenomenology of religion'. *Journal of the American Academy of Religion*, 53(1): 51–73.

INDEX

www.ingramcontent.com/pod-product-compliance
Ingram Content Group UK Ltd.
Pitfield, Milton Keynes, MK11 3LW, UK
UKHW020736280225
455688UK00012B/693